Table of Contents

Dedication

For Edith and Cj Stevens, with affection and gratitude.

Six One-Act Farces

Albert Bermel

ORACLE
PRESS

Oracle Press takes pleasure in presenting this, the fourth in a series of volumes of plays and books relating to the Theatre.

The three preceeding books are: *Three Plays by Louisiana Playwrights, Corrugated Scenery,* and translations of Racine's *Phaedre* and *Iphigenia.*

Solemn Introduction

*These plays are presented here in the order in which they were writ-
ten between 1961 and 1972. The reader will notice that they advance
(or retreat) from near-realism to near-abstraction. At first I wanted to
find out whether I could tell a fairly straightforward anecdote. Later I
wanted not to have to. The early ones distantly derive from actual
happenings — to myself or somebody else. The later ones don't. For
all six a measure of realistic conviction will improve the playing. In
farce, as in other kinds of theatre, the characters take one another
seriously. During one attempt in a far-off spot at* The Adjustment *I
didn't hear anything about the results. Some time afterward I met the
downcast actress. She'd felt uncomfortable in this two-character play.
I'd loaded her up with too much to say; the role, a soliloquy with in-
terruptions, had forced her partner, the actor, to stand around like a
dummy and take care not to upstage her. Startled by this 18th-century
interpretation, the director's, no doubt, I mentioned what I'd thought
was obvious, that her speeches were anything but soliloquies: they
were intended to harangue and ensnare the other character, not the
audience, and he was supposed to resist being harangued and
ensnared. She turned away and said, "Oh, my God!" In another stag-
ing, which I did see, a different actress brought to the same role a
heartfelt pathos that took me by delighted surprise because she didn't
strain for it and didn't sacrifice any of the humor. Here, too, the
director must have had a critical hand, only this time a constructive
one.*

A number of productions have been done in remote places. I'd have dearly liked to witness **The Workout** *in Tokyo,* **The Recovery** *in Edinburgh,* **The Adjustment** *at Spoleto, and similar exotica. Each new showing with a different cast and director and designer is, after all, a fresh slant, almost a new play, for in the theatre nothing is obvious. Every play has ridiculous elasticity. A playwright never knows what he has written. Even when it confronts him on stage after stage he catches mere glimpses of its possibilities, which may not correspond to that astigmatic vision of enactment he once had. Some showings will make it look better than the vision, some worse. In any case, he doesn't see them all, and perhaps that's just as well, otherwise he might start imitating himself. Who has the time, the money, and the egomaniacal resolve to chase every play down every avenue of realization? And how is it possible to subdivide oneself when different stagings occur in the same month? Usually he orphans his scripts for the moment, sends them out into the darkness of playhouses, and prays for a happy landing.*

I thank the theatre artists who have taken chances with these plays, have sometimes given them sturdy limbs, strong voices, unashamedly farcical spirits, and, in a few cases, wings.

A.B.

The Workout

LES, a flab
MARGE, a girl

DOC FINNEY'S in Midtown Manhattan, a gymnasium under fluo-rescent lighting. The floor may be wooden but the wood is covered by wine-red, wall-to-wall carpeting. Bars and chromium-plated weights are arranged by sizes on racks built into the rear wall. A desk and two chairs are set in front. A man in a business suit comes through the doorway. He touches the carpet, appreciating its texture and thick-ness. He picks up one of the weights, is surprised to see how light it is, smiles, and raises it playfully above his head. He picks up another weight of the same size in his other hand, raises it too, and marches around the gymnasium with both weights high, laughing. He puts the weights back and tries two heavier ones. With difficulty he gets them up above his head and begins to march around the room again, but is forced to stop and lower them. After a rest and three deep breaths he tries to raise the weights again, but cannot. He takes a deeper breath and tries again, raises the weights, but has to put them down again im-mediately. He takes off his jacket, hangs it on the rack, removes his cuff links and rolls up his shirt sleeves.

With a tremendous jerk he raises the weights again and carries them back to the rack, running-staggering the last few paces, and letting them fall almost out of control. He stands panting for a few seconds, then collects his jacket and puts it on again. He straightens his tie, wipes his forehead and palms with the handkerchief from his breast pocket.

1

MAN. Beautiful carpet. Beautiful weights. *(Raps a weight with his knuckle.)* Pre-war chrome. *(A girl comes through the door. She is wearing a white blouse, monogrammed with a curly D.F., white socks and sneakers.)*

MAN. My friend Raymond says once you can raise weights you can do anything, go anywhere. Moving up, he says, is taking on one weight after another, getting stronger all the time, until you hoist the largest ones. I don't agree with that. Seems to me it's better to know which weights to lift and which weights to leave alone.

GIRL. I'm Marge.

MAN. I'm Les.

MARGE. This your first time at Doc Finney's?

LES. Well, I've seen your ads and your commercials. And the girl in your showroom on 57th Street. A knockout, that one. So is the showroom.

MARGE. But this is your first actual visit?

LES. My friend Raymond invited me. He's a member. He said I could be his guest.

MARGE. Every member is allowed one free guest a week.

LES. He said we could meet for a workout, instead of wasting our lunch hour eating.

MARGE. More and more people are making good use of their lunch hours.

LES. My friend Raymond will be here soon.

MARGE. We can start without waiting for him.

LES. Just the two of us?

MARGE. We'll give you the limber-up for neophytes.

LES. Just so I don't wake up in the morning with a charlie horse.

MARGE. Did they show you the locker rooms?

LES. That's where I'm supposed to meet Raymond.

MARGE. You'll see him.

LES. Thanks.

MARGE. Do you have any sneakers?

LES. Not with me. Thanks, anyway. I like the feel of the red carpet. Gives pleasure to the feet.

MARGE. It should, at fifty slammers a yard. Mohair and vicuna, a special blend made up for Doc Finney. But it's not for feet. It's for sneakers. That'll be 20 dollars even.

LES. I thought the workout came for free.

MARGE. Plus you have to wear the T-shirt and shorts in the hall of worship. Doc Finney's regulations. Forty-one-seventy-five. Pay now, please.

LES. Couldn't I just take off my jacket and tie?

MARGE. Doc Finney says T-shirts and shorts. For the sake of the other members of the congregation. Sixty-one-seventy-five altogether. *(She hands him the gym wear, takes his wallet from his hand, and counts out the bills.)* I owe you a quarter.

LES. Keep it.

MARGE. What d'you think I am, a waitress? I owe you a quarter, I said. Okay. Strip down.

LES. Here?

MARGE. Here and now. Don't throw those blushes at me. I've seen it all.

LES. Don't you have a cubicle or a screen?

MARGE. This is not a men's wear store. Come on, now.

LES. As long as you're not embarrassed . . . *(She laughs.)* Could you turn away a little?

MARGE. Why? *(He gives in. Bent almost double, he fumbles off his trousers and undershorts and tries to draw the shorts up under his long-tailed shirt.)* Do you need a hand?

LES. No; no thanks.

MARGE. Hurry up with the T-shirt.

LES. I'm trying to. *(He gets the T-shirt stuck across his head and shoulders. She pulls it down for him. He jumps.)* Thanks.

MARGE. We'll get rid of these clothes and then we're ready. *(She bundles up the clothes and throws them into the cupboard.)* First, we'll fill out your progress card.

LES. Progress in what?

MARGE. Your development.

LES. How can I progress if I'm not coming back?

MARGE. We'll talk about that after the measurements. *(She leads him to the desk.)*

LES. You're going to measure me? *(He moves away.)*

MARGE. Are you frightened?

LES. Who, me?

3

MARGE. *(Reading from the card.)* How often did you speak to the Lord in the last year?

LES. You need an exact answer? *(She nods.)* None.

MARGE. I could have guessed that from looking at you.

LES. Does it really show?

MARGE. Straighten your back. That's **better.** You rose three inches nearer to Heaven when you did that. Have you **ever** spoken to the Lord?

LES. Once or twice. You know the kind of thing. I said, "Oh, God, get me out of this." Funny thing — He usually did. But I don't know if I was really talking to Him or who the heck it was.

MARGE. Did you go down on your knees?

LES. I have a varicose vein.

MARGE. *(Writing.)* No knees. How many times a week do you read your Bible?

LES. For enjoyment or for real?

MARGE. Either way.

LES. I don't have a Bible.

MARGE. *(Getting him a Bible from the closet)* Take care of that. Show a little reverence for it. Kiss it.

LES. *(Kissing)* Thanks.

MARGE. Twenty-nine-ninety-five, please.

LES. Jesus, I can buy me a Bible for less than thirty bucks.

MARGE. Not with this binding. We have this edition made up for us. Resists scuffing. Take it into the shower. Use it for a doorstop. Chop wood on it. The Doc Finney revised version. *(He has taken out his wallet. She removes more bills.)* I owe you thirty cents. So, what do you do on Sundays?

LES. Sleep.

MARGE. You never meditate?

LES. I got nothing much to meditate about.

MARGE. You will by the time I get finished with you. Here's a text for you to meditate next Sunday. "Did you swear at anybody? Did you insult anybody? Did you shout at anybody?" That's Kings, Book Two, verse twenty-two. You meditate that. You memorize it.

LES. Did I shout at somebody? Did I bawl out somebody? Doesn't sound like the Bible to me, what I've heard of the Bible.

MARGE. I told you: it's Doc Finney's revised version. *(She finds the*

4

place in his copy and turns the corner down. He is muttering the verses to himself.) Don't meditate yet. That's for Sunday. I'm going to give you a text for now.

LES. Great. *(She goes to the rack, with him following, takes two small weights, lifts them above her head and proceeds to straighten and bend her knees as she chants.)*

MARGE. Raise me up, O Lord, Cast me down, O God. Raise me up, O Lord. Cast me down, O God. Get it?

LES. You have beautiful leg muscles.

MARGE. Your turn. Face the altar. *(She turns him toward the weight rack.)*

LES. *(Descending.)* Cast me down, O —

MARGE. Not yet. Wait till you start to come up. Now: Raise me —

LES. — Up, O Lord. Cast me down, O God. Raise me up, O God. Cast me down, O Lord. Up, O Lord. Down, O God. Oh, God, I don't think I can get up again. Raise me, O Lord, for Christ's sake. *(Straining.)* I made it.

MARGE. With God's help.

LES. And I guess Doc Finney's. Shall I try one more?. I'm getting the swing nicely now.

MARGE. No.

LES. I can.

MARGE. And cats can bark.

LES. I'm stronger than I look.

MARGE. That I can believe.

LES. What comes next?

MARGE. We'll take five while you recover. *(She leads him back to the desk.)* Before you know where you are, you'll be in a state of grace. But first let's find out more about you. *(They sit down.)*

LES. Next, you plan to ask me what church I don't go to.

MARGE. Before I ask you some more, I want to tell you a few facts about Doc Finney's. This is the small hall for novices. Dedication One-A. The larger hall for advanced courses is one flight up: Two-A, Three-A and Sacraments. It's equipped with every sideline you can think of.

LES. Pews?

MARGE. Twelve pews in oiled oak, imported from Britain.

LES. Kneeling mats?

5

MARGE. Jute kneeling mats from India, with foam rubber lining.

LES. Where does the foam rubber come from?

MARGE. Keep the questions sacred.

LES. Um — Candles?

MARGE. Every size and color of candle. Made in Hong Kong to Doc Finney's long-burning specifications.

LES. Candlesticks?

MARGE. Gigantic candlesticks in pink gold. Most of them are bigger and heavier than you. What else can you think of?

LES. I've run out of ideas.

MARGE. Doc Finney hasn't. We have a nave and chapel designed in plastic mahogany by a famous Swedish guy you probably never heard of. Take it apart, it fits into your briefcase. You feel like praying, it assembles in fifteen seconds flat. We have West German stained-glass windows from West Germany — real ancient style, and strictly for Old Testament movie fans. Adam and Eve in the raw, Susannah in the kidney-shaped Esther Williams lake, Sodom, Gomorrah, crucifixions galore. You name it. We have sculptures in marbleite sculpted just the way the Italian sculptors used to sculpt.

LES. If they *look* the same . . .

MARGE. We have every piece of equipment needed to — in Doc Finney's well-known words — to maximize your faith. Ask your parson. Ask your priest. Ask your rabbi. Ask your mullah. Notice I don't ask your religion. We're inter-denominational here. Doesn't make a speck of difference which God you believe in. You walk into Doc Finney's with your head low, but when you walk out you stand right, look right, breathe right and stay right.

LES. My friend Raymond has picked up some of that jargon. He was saying . . .

MARGE. After each workout you sing the hymn for the day with your instructor, who has a Ph.D. in physical theology. Then you dive into a mud bath and an alcohol rinse. You sit in the Caribbean sunlight room under twelve 500-watt units. When the gong goes you wash away your sweat and sin in the Mediterranean stall showers. Cobalt-tinted glass. Then you dress in the largest locker rooms in the world. Every one has a built-in bar with push-button scotch at your own ready-mixed proof. Our locker-room nurses are lay preachers. You choose your favorite brand of after-shave lotion and talcum powder **or** your favorite blessing. We have a list of one thousand selected

6

blessings, all the way from "Make me simple" to "Make me smart." What are you staring at my knees for? Haven't you ever seen a pair of woman's knees?

LES. Oh, sure. Several times. I was just thinking: kneeling has done your knees a lot of good.

MARGE. You should see what it's done to my morale. So, your name is Les. Is that short for Lester?

LES. No, Leslie.

MARGE. Leslie? That's a girl's name.

LES. These days any man's name is a girl's name. Tracy and Brett and Lindsay and Hilton and Tammy and Dale. And the men have women's names like Connie and Claire and Sal and Shirley and Joyce. I used to know an awful lot about names and sex. Phineas means serpent's mouth. I had a buddy called Phineas. Every time he opened his jaws we used to say, "Stow it, Snaky" and he'd get mad and . . .

MARGE. Have you finished? It's your lunch hour you're wasting. Now, your given name is Leslie. Leslie — a man? Crazy. What's your surname?

LES. If I tell you, you'll look up my address in the phone directory and keep sending me brochures.

MARGE. Who needs the phone directory? Give me your address next.

LES. My big mouth . . .

MARGE. I must have a name for the progress report. Or how will we know who is progressing?

LES. Is it all right if I give you a false name?

MARGE. We'll come back to your name and address. How old are you?

LES. Forty-one.

MARGE. Forty-**one**?

LES. Forty-five.

MARGE. That's nearer. Are there any physical or mental defects in your family?

LES. Only pigeon toes.

MARGE. Some of our top athletes and scholars used to have pigeon toes. Not now. Doc Finney took care of that.

LES. I wouldn't say I was much of an athlete. Or a scholar.

MARGE. *(Standing.)* Nor would I. Get up. We have real work to do on you.

7

LES. *(Standing.)* What kind of work?

MARGE. Stripping away all that flabbiness. Firming you up. You're a flab.

LES. Where?

MARGE. Up and down. All over. Most people are flabs when they start. Some development you have. Look at that midsection. Look at that chest. Look at that pot. Look at those crummy triceps. Flab, flab, flab. I wouldn't even take your measurements. They'd be unreliable. You're too shaky. We'll have to put a pair of shoulders on you. We'll have to fill you with humbleness and pride.

LES. At the same time?

MARGE. We'll have to give you lungs to shout God's praises with, and arms to pray with. We'll have to straighten out your back. You're all droopy and stoopy. A man should get up to his height so he can look God in the eye and say, "Hello, God. I'm Les." Sit down.

LES. I was trying to get up to my height, but it's too high for me . . .

MARGE. *(Writing.)* Are you married?

LES. Yes.

MARGE. You are?

LES. Why are you so surprised?

MARGE. I'm surprised a woman puts up with a development like yours.

LES. She never notices it. We have concealed lighting in the bedroom.

MARGE. Was that your idea?

LES. No, hers.

MARGE. That figures.

LES. She never complains to me.

MARGE. I'll bet. I'll bet she's cried herself to sleep more times than you know. You see, it isn't just God. It's your wife too. Wouldn't you like your wife to respect you?

LES. It doesn't much matter either way. We have three children.

MARGE. Don't you want to be admired by other people?

LES. What sort of other people?

MARGE. Women.

LES. That's something else.

MARGE. When a woman passes you in the street or sees you standing on the beach or digging into a file cabinet in your office, she should be able to say: "That's a man."

LES. What else could she say?

MARGE. She wouldn't say a thing. She wouldn't even see you. If you want to be seen you have to make the most of what God has given you.

LES. It sounds hopeless. I'm too far gone to catch up with the human race. Look what a handicap I have: no church, no faith, no meditation. Just pigeon toes and flab.

MARGE. That's defeatism. And, as Doc Finney says, defeatism is unhealthy, ungodly and un-American. The day will come — you have work to do, but it'll come — when you walk out of here with maximum faith. Like all the others.

LES. What if I'm different from all the others? With minimum faith?

MARGE. Come over here, wiseacre. You've had your rest. *(She takes him to the rack.)* We'll see if we can save you. Let's start the second part of your workout. I want you to stretch your arms. *(She stands like a cross, to show him. He imitates her. She puts a weight into each hand.)* Take up your burdens. Now repeat the second text, ten times: "Teach me to live upright in thy sight."

LES. Teach me to —

MARGE. Hold it. Your arms are sagging. Chest out, chin back, arms like rods. Upright. Okay, again.

LES. **Teach** me to live upright in thy sight. Teach **me** to live upright in thy sight. Teach me to **live** — I feel like I'm dying. *(Rushing.)* Teach -me-to-live-upright-in-thy-sight. Wow. *(Drops his arms.)* That's my limit.

MARGE. You see how far you have to go? You barely made four out of ten. Burdens down. Back on to the altar neatly. Take five breaths to relax. In, out. In, out. In, out. Now sit down again. *(He sits on the floor.)* I want to ask you some personal questions. Have you ever had trouble with your conscience?

LES. Yes.

MARGE. I knew it.

LES. Especially before and after meals. I tell myself: Les, you ought to —

MARGE. I'm talking about your conscience, your heart.

LES. I get pains there too. Let's face it, I'm forty-nine — forty-five.

MARGE. Have you ever felt afraid?

LES. All the time. I get lonely, mostly when I'm alone. I ask myself what it's all about.

MARGE. I'll tell you why. A spirit in your condition is sick. It's liable to trap every suspicion and evil that floats past a healthy spirit. And as you get older that sickness will become a disease. Ingrown. You think you're unhappy now, when you get an attack of conscience that lasts for two minutes. Wait till it lasts for an hour, a week, a year. Wait till the time comes when you're never free of that conscience. Are you listening to me?

LES. *(Looking about.)* Yes. I was wondering if my friend Raymond has arrived.

MARGE. Your friend Raymond must be in the upper hall of worship. How advanced is he? Has he got as far as Ritual Release?

LES. Who knows? He's a 24-carat kook. Did he have to go through the conscience bit?

MARGE. Ask him yourself. Find out how much good it did him.

LES. It sure took a time. He's been coming here for two years.

MARGE. He must be working out thoroughly. What kind of a course does he have?

LES. What kinds are there?

MARGE. I'm glad you asked me that question. There are three courses: A-plus, B-extra and C-major. You can't go wrong on any of them. In Doc Finney's words, they're all package deals and every package is gift-wrapped.

LES. I can't afford them.

MARGE. You don't have to. For you there's a special offer —

LES. Don't tell me. I have no money with me. I don't want any packages or offers. I want to see my friend Raymond and grab my clothes and get out of here.

MARGE. Sit down. I'm not sure if the special offer is still in force. Maybe we can make an exception and extend it just for you. I'm going out to have a word with Doc Finney. *(She goes out and locks the door behind her. LES goes swiftly to the closet, takes out his clothes, starts to put them on, decides that will take him too long, throws them over his arm and makes for the door. Before he reaches it, MARGE returns.)*

MARGE. Put those clothes back. It's all set up. You're lucky. Today is the last day. You made it just in time. Very sneaky. These are the terms of the special offer . . .

LES. It sounds good to me. Wrap it up and hold it for me. I'll let you have a check in a few days.

MARGE. I didn't make myself clear. This offer expires today . . . ends, finishes, concludes, terminates.

LES. *(Helpfully.)* Dies.

MARGE. You don't think this one over. In a few days it'll be a few days too late. I'm not about to pressure you into anything. Doc Finney doesn't go for pressure. Well?

LES. You're not with it, are you?

MARGE. What do you mean?

LES. I mean, you don't have much of a pitch.

MARGE. Who are you to criticize? If you weren't a customer — a convert — I'd tell you . . .

LES. I'm no customer, Marge. I happen to be — and listen to me with both ears, Marge, because you fell into a lot of bloopers today — I happen to be New York Sales Manager for a mattress firm. **The** mattress. Marge, you wouldn't last two days on my sales force.

MARGE. Are you stacking God up against mattresses?

LES. Oh, I don't say they're exactly the same kind of merchandise. But Marge, have you got a lot to learn. That hard sell. Billy Sunday. Look, the nineteen-thirties are down the drain. Marge, I'm going to show you how you can put some box spring into your selling, so that your prospects really bounce. This is what I tell the boys: Don't be satisfied to push mattresses; make believe they're trampolines. Whing, whang. The same goes for you.

MARGE. Mockery! You're making fun of God.

LES. You can't make fun of something you don't understand. I'll be frank with you, Marge. I don't understand mattresses. Not one bit. What is a mattress? Steel, wood, fabric? Maybe. But it's also comfort. That's something I understand. So that's what I sell. A benefit. A specific. And that's what you should sell. God's comfort. You started handing me that phony-baloney about being a flab and not kneeling and does my wife cry in bed. Meadow dressing. I was leading you on. I was playing the wide-eyed mark. Nifty, hey? Now, Marge, once I thought you'd hit your stride when you said did I want to be appealing to women. But you rolled away from that. You talked about consciences and heartaches. Negative selling. Quackery. All the time you should have been zeroing in on me with benefits you kept unloading fears. Another five minutes, you'd've had me in the middle of Danton's Inferno. Is that a way to part a man and his money? Forget it.

11

Forget about after-shave and talcum and the rest of the perfume grind. That's all for pansies, and never mind what the ads tell you. Besides, I'm asking myself, "How much is that smelly hullaballoo adding to my ticket?" And quoting this bird Doc Finney. That's the corniest angle of all. There isn't any Doc Finney, is there?

MARGE. He's not exactly a doctor . . .

LES. Who gives a hoot what kind of a stiff he is? I'm dealing with you. Every time you tell me Doc Finney says this or that you sabotage your authority.

MARGE. I've only been here three weeks.

LES. How many sales you made?

MARGE. One.

LES. An old guy?

MARGE. Yes.

LES. See? Hard selling only makes it with the old folks. Even some of them have wised up. The insurance boys have hammered it into the ground. Too bad, Marge. As a saleslady you're no go. *(He stands back and watches her. She puts down her head and weeps.)* Cut that out. Crying is the worst approach of all. What good can it do? It can only make the prospect nervous. And nervous is what you don't want him to be. He has to be: one, confident; two, excited.

MARGE. How do you make him confident?

LES. I'm coming to that. Now. You're on a commission deal, right? And one commission in three weeks is rough, right?

MARGE. I owe money.

LES. Sure you do. You need every sale you can pull. You got to round up those commissions. So your mind has to be nimble, dancing on twinkle toes. You have to build up a vision. Not just God: something bigger.

MARGE. How?

LES. By personalizing every interview. For you that's easy.

MARGE. Why?

LES. You have a powerful come-on. I'm talking about your looks. You're a pretty girl, a very pretty girl. And you're built. You realize that?

MARGE. Some people tell me I'm all right . . .

LES. Just so you're aware of it. Marge, your looks are why you were hired. Selling, let's face it, is another word for seduction. Rape, even. For instance, you show me how to pray. Put my hands together. *(She*

12

does.) Not like a dummy. Slowly, lovingly. Like a woman. *(She tries again.)* Better. Much better. That gives me goose pimples. And every last goose pimple is selling for you. Now you say, "Les, you have natural faith."

MARGE. Les, you have natural faith.

LES. Let's see more passion. More sincerity.

MARGE. Les, **you** have natural **faith.**

LES. Now you're convincing me. I'm getting confident. But before I get over-confident and figure what do I need courses for if I already have faith, you say: "But in three weeks you can be a saint."

MARGE. In three weeks you can be a saint.

LES. Swell. Don't give me that woolly hocus-pocus about maximums. Lay the benefits on the line. Me — a saint — in just three weeks. John, Matthew, Mark, Lucas, Francis of Sicily, Shakespeare, Albert Schweitzer, Jesus. Me. I think and my mind whirls. But maybe I come from Missouri. I stop whirling long enough to say: "But I'm thirty-five." Then you come right back with: "Thirty-five is the most amazing age of all. At thirty-five, men have conquered mountains. They've been heavyweight champions of the world. They've sold articles to the magazines. They've walked clean across the United States in **galoshes.**" You follow what I'm aiming at? I'm talking specifics.

MARGE. Suppose you ask me what mountains men have conquered at thirty-five?

LES. You come back quick as a bullet with the names of a few good mountains.

MARGE. I don't know any.

LES. Marge, you got to do your homework. You have to be ready to substantiate. Mount Sinai, you say. And if they ask you what swimming records, you flash out, "The quarter mile freestyle," and you add, "One minute, seventeen and a half seconds." Is anybody going to contradict you?

MARGE. You might, if you're an expert.

LES. You're the expert. Besides, you've just come up close to me again. You're brushing my shoulder and reminding me that in two weeks I'll double my virtue.

MARGE. *(Cooing.)* In two weeks you'll double your virtue.

LES. Specifics again. Not I'll increase it. I'll double it. You're giving me the Vision. Now. You take me by the hand. *(Giving her his hand.)* You act a little flirty. It's all part of the game. That's what you're here for. And you make the most of your assets. *(Takes her in his arms and*

13

kisses her.) Very fine. Assets all the way. You lead me over to the altar — here — and you show me the way to heaven. *(They pick up a weight.)* You bend forward with me — with me, not away from me — so we're touching. Just a little of the business. Enough but not too much. And you put your tiny little hand over mine and we take up our burdens and start rising together. Up, up, up. You're not as tall as me, so you let your hand slide down to my elbow. A scrap of mischief, that's all. Does nobody any harm and makes me feel real good. More goose pimples; more benefits. I relax one second, and I say, "Can I ask you a question?" You say, "Yes."

MARGE. Yes.

LES. And I say, "What're you doing tonight?" And you say, "I'm staying home."

MARGE. I'm staying home.

LES. And I say, "How's about coming to church?" And you say, "You said you were going to ask me one question, not two."

MARGE. One question, not two.

LES. But you don't want to disappoint me. You break in with, "Maybe we can deal with the second question later."

MARGE. *(Excited.)* Second question later.

LES. Ha! We're coming up toward the excitement bit. So far you've achieved plenty. I've started the workout. You've got me confident. We've talked about a date and you haven't dismissed it, only postponed it. Now you're going to **prove** to me that I was born to die holy. You say, "Try the ritual ten times."

MARGE. Yes. I mean, try the ritual ten times.

LES. *(Lifting.)* One, two, three, four, five, six, seven, eight, nine, ten. Forget about the text for the time being. That confuses me. Then I say, "Shall I try another five?" and you say — putting an awful lot of astonishment into your voice — "Do you think you can?"

MARGE. Do you **think** you **can**?

LES. That's it. Flatter me out of my goddam wits. *(Panting.)* Before, I couldn't get up to God four times. Now: ten, fifteen, any number. I'm swelling with pride. And humbleness. Both. I'm almost sold. The commission is in the bag for you. *(Lifting again with increasing difficulty.)* Eleven, twelve, thirteen, fourteen, fifteen. What a man. What a saint. Encourage me. Encourage the hell out of me. *(She kisses him again.)* Tremendous. Sixteen, seventeen, eighteen, nineteen, twenty. I did it. I hit twenty. *(Puts down the weight.)* So here I am, breathing hard, but half-holy. Bursting with sainthood. You're admiring me with every damn feature in your pretty face. I stand up very straight. You've given me the Vision. I'm sold. I'M SOLD!

MARGE. *(After a pause, slowly.)* But if you're a salesman wouldn't you be too skeptical to — Les, is something wrong?

LES. I — no. Got a little dizzy. I guess all that holiness must have been too . . . I'm sold . . . I . . . *(He collapses. She drags him to the wall and props him against it. He blinks a few times.)*

MARGE. Sit there, Les. Don't move, darling. You hear me?

LES. All that . . . holiness . . .

MARGE. Les! You did great. Where's your wallet? *(Takes it from his pocket.)* You're qualified to go right into C-major. Oh, too bad: only fifty bucks here. Let's call it a deposit. Fifty down and forty-nine fifties to come. You know what, Les? I'd say you're in a state of grace. You bounced into it. Whing, whang. Somehow, Les, you made it the quick way.

Dimout

15

The Adjustment

MRS. GROAT, a flooded subject
MR. FESTER, the adjuster

MRS. GROAT is untidying up in her basement. This spacious room, the length and breadth of the suburban house above it, has been converted to a den or playroom by the expenditure of love, labors, cost. But the set should draw it stylistically, sparely, with no attempt at accuracy. Mrs. Groat tips some of the contents of a can of paint against the wall and pours the remainder with a flourish on the rug. She eases a couple of plywood panels away from the brickwork behind them. She splits one of the panels with an axe. She saws at the legs on a table. She punches artistic dents in a lampshade and bends the stem of the lamp until it stands at an angle to the base. She takes a mop and dabs at an untidy patch in the ceiling; some rubble descends.

Every few seconds she consults her watch, and looks up at a doorway at the top of a flight of steps. When her work is finished she pauses to scan the room. Are there any parts of it she has not mistreated? Yes, the door itself.

She charges up the steps with her mop held as a lance, and shatters the lower left section. A sound of human damage comes from the other side of the door. She opens it. A man stands in view, a formally dressed, undertakerish man, holding his right shin.

16

MRS. GROAT: You're here, you're here! You're Mr. Fester.

MR. FESTER: *(Straightening up)* In person.

MRS. GROAT: From the insurance company.

MR. FESTER: May it prosper.

MRS. GROAT: Me too. You came to see Mrs. Groat with one *t* and no *e*.

MR. FESTER: *(Consulting a form)* One *t*, no *e*.

MRS. GROAT: It's me, Mrs. Groat. So help me if I was expecting you.

MR. FESTER: I believe I am exactly on time.

MRS. GROAT: That's a gorgeous tie you got on, Mr. Fester. Excuse me for noticing. I like black around a man's neck. Or any color. Cheers up that part of the body.

MR. FESTER: May I come in?

MRS. GROAT: Mrs. Belinda Groat. My dearest friends call me Sugar. You can guess why. The place is a mess. What do you do after a disaster? I'm sorry if I broke your leg.

MR. FESTER: It's a little crowded up here. May I go down?

MRS. GROAT: I tried to clean up. I wanted it to be, you know, presentable. I didn't have a soul to turn to, Mr. Fester, except my sister, and catch her showing anybody a kind hand. Can you believe that, Mr. Fester, her own sister? My mother used to say she was born without a heart. Not with a small heart. Without one. Don't be a stranger, Mr. Fester. You don't have to be standoffish with Sugar Groat. *(She hold out her hands. He edges past her politely and comes down the steps.)* You know how it is: you have a guest coming. You want to make things nice, even if he's only the insurance man. Excuse me for saying only.

MR. FESTER: The adjuster.

MRS. GROAT: So you finally came. After a week you made it. I'm happy at least it wasn't somebody else. Even if I don't know you, I like sympathetic, good-looking people. I get along with them. You tell your company from me I appreciate it. I enjoy a person a person can talk to. What only went on in this playroom. I'm so ashamed. Did they tell you I was under four feet six of water?

MR. FESTER: The precise depth doesn't concern me.

MRS. GROAT: Four-eight. Eight, not six. It went up to ten or eleven if you made waves. I said to my sister, "What some people would give to have an indoor pool like this in their playroom." She didn't crack a

17

smile. Doesn't have my sense of humor. A gorgon. You know what a gorgon is?

MR. FESTER: Where is the water now?

MRS. GROAT: It drained away. It's probably working at the foundations. Who knows? The whole house could topple any second. If I give you the word, run.

MR. FESTER: You drained it away yourself?

MRS. GROAT: Me? I didn't touch a thing. I know the rules. I read my policy. The fine print too. I enjoy a good policy. Better than the accident pages in the paper. I'm not joking. There it was: here. A regular Lake Superior. First thing I thought was: Try the dehumidifier. But. Look at it — a seventy-four-fifty dehumidifier, drowned. So I thought: I'll rescue what I can. *(Comes down the steps slowly, takes off her shoes, tries her toe in the "water.")* Icy. It was supposed to be a hot water pipe had busted. You'd never know it. More than anything else, my toes are sensitive to the cold. *(She descends two more steps, "splashing" her legs, and shivering. She takes another step down.)* I should've worn my swimsuit. **But.** My valise is put away with my swimsuit in it. It's the two-piece type, you know, with a halter on top and white stitching which says, "Hands off." That's a joke. But unpack it when it was already packed? Not on your oath, Mr. Fester. I had to make do. Quick as a zipper I slipped into my old white rayon blouse. And my cream shorts. They have a vertical stripe. Very lovely. I took one dip and ruined them. *(She "swims" across the room.)* The cold, the cold. I could've gone in naked as a swordfish, it would still have taken every inch of feeling out of my body. Excuse me for being suggestive. *(She "swims" back to the steps.)* The shorts are another item will have to go on your estimate. New the end of last season. Size 12. Cream. *(She walks down the steps into the room.)* Excuse me if I push you out of the way. It's that you're in the way. So the man came to fix the pipe. And I fixed him. But good. I mean, they waltz in, they put a dab of something on the leak, they show you a bill it's so high you could get a hernia just looking at it. From one little pipe, ruination. Well, slowly the tide went out. That's a joke. I mean, it was cold water and it was supposed to come from a hot pipe. You ought to have seen the water mark it left on the wall.

MR. FESTER: You engaged a man to drain away the water?

MRS. GROAT: I told you: It drained itself, gurgling like crazy. That gurgling kept me up nights. Each morning I measured it. I took a tape measure, I held the end of the tape measure between my big toes with my feet together. Four feet what did I say? Ten inches, including waves.

MR. FESTER: I don't see any water mark.

MRS. GROAT: You know how it is. Don't make me for a liar, Mr. Fester. I have nothing to hide. The water marks got washed away by the water. And with all that mud and earth out there that came in from my flower beds! All my asters and lobelias — murdered. I'm not joking.

MR. FESTER: Here? I see no trace of mud.

MRS. GROAT: Not there. There. Everywhere. A damp disaster.

MR. FESTER: Why did you clean up?

MRS. GROAT: All I did to the water was when it had died down my sister and I took mops and worked at the mud. Two hard days of mopping. My sister: I gave her a mop, she leaned on it. You talk about the wall. Never mind water marks. Look what it did to my oak paneling. *(She seizes a panel, fights with it, finally succeeds in tugging it away.)* The whole thing is falling apart. Next, you'll tell me the oak looks like plywood.

MR. FESTER: Not at all.

MRS. GROAT: You were just going to. I could see your lips making the word —

MR. FESTER: I suggest my lips are under perfect control.

MRS. GROAT: Not in a million years. Plywood is plywood, Mr. Fester. Oak is more robust. Would I put in twenty-cents-a-foot plywood in a playroom that cost this much to set up? Don't write yet. Don't write a thing.

MR. FESTER: I'm not writing.

MRS. GROAT: I have plenty to show you, Mr. Fester, you and your insurance company. If you'll just step off my carpeting.

MR. FESTER: Your rug?

MRS. GROAT: What are you calling a rug? My wool carpeting? If it looks like cotton that's because of the soaking it took. Why are you tapping your foot? Testing it? You don't believe it's not cotton?

MR. FESTER: Wool, cotton. These are trivial distinctions.

MRS. GROAT: Trivial did you say? See those wool loops? The finest Persian wool. Take a look at the backing.

MR. FESTER: *(Fingering the backing)* It certainly is backing.

MRS. GROAT: The heaviest rubber. After the water the loops came unlooped. That's why you called it cotton. I wouldn't dare tell you

19

what I paid for that English wool carpeting. I would never have been able to afford it except they featured it in the year-end sale with up to forty-five per cent off. You buy the best it gives you security. And that's what we all want, Mr. Fester, don't we? That's what insurance policies are for. That poor, dead Persian carpeting. And **then** what happened to it?

MR. FESTER: The paint?

MRS. GROAT: A gallon of fresh paint. Another item for your estimate.

MR. FESTER: Where did the paint leak from?

MRS. GROAT: You're asking me questions. You're trying to outsmart me. That I don't go for, Mr. Fester. Beware of me when I get suspicious. The paint tipped. An entire can of new paint. Must have been the force of the water. Come here. Did you notice what happened to this lamp? A wedding gift, a treasure.

MR. FESTER: The paint on the rug — on the carpeting — is still wet.

MRS. GROAT: Can you wonder?

MR. FESTER: But after a week?

MRS. GROAT: Don't blame me if it took you a week to arrive. Some drenching I went through in this place.

MR. FESTER: How did the paint get here, Mrs. *(He looks at the form.)* Groat?

MRS. GROAT: I knew you'd ask that. I was ready for that question. You won't trip Belinda Groat. The contractor left it. A contractor, a crook. He had to have that extra can of paint. I told him, four cans is enough. He needed five. Wise guy. He gets up too early.

MR. FESTER: Paintwork? In this room?

MRS. GROAT: Go argue with a contractor. I'm not joking. They'll paint you out of house and home. Mr. Fester, you have no idea how much invisible work goes into a playroom. And what kind of play am I getting out of it now? *(She prods the ceiling. A tile falls. She hands it to him.)* What would you say that ceiling's made of?

MR. FESTER: Cork?

MRS. GROAT: The finest cork. And like a cork it popped. You'll tell me it's very thin for cork.

MR. FESTER: I suppose it is.

MRS. GROAT: What do you mean, thin? You have to have your cork thin. If it's thick it muffles the sound.

MR. FESTER: Isn't that what cork's for?

20

MRS. GROAT: Listen to me. I'll give you a quick lesson in cork. You think I want one of those playrooms where you can sit in silence and a horse and buggy could drive through the kitchen and toilet right above us and you wouldn't hear a murmur? A person wants to get away from things but she wants to know what's taking place in her own upstairs. Private she wants to be, ignorant no. That's the quality cork I had there. You could tile the roof of the Pacific ocean with that cork. I'm talking about the price. Now look. Shriveled. *(She goes at the ceiling with the axe handle. More tiles fall.)* This is a game room, I said? I wouldn't even show you the Monopoly board. Thousands of dollars stuck together. Every stitch of property in ruins. Now take a quick look at the ping pong table, instead of leaning on it. Did you ever see a ping pong table in such a state? *(She thumps it.)*

MR. FESTER: Mrs. *(He looks at the form.)* Groat, I owe you an explanation.

MRS. GROAT: That's not all you owe me. I haven't started yet. Thank God for insurance. Come here; you're standing too close to the warps. The table is covered in warps. I'll bet you thought it had measles. *(She hands him a paddle, takes a ball from her apron, and runs to the other side of the table.)* Service! *(He watches the ball go past.)* Ha, what did I tell you? It hit a warp.

MR. FESTER: I don't play this game.

MRS. GROAT: What a smash you missed because of that warp. I have a weak serve. You would have finished me. Not only warps. How about this? *(She takes a knife from her apron and peels a strip from the surface of the table.)* Coming away worse than sunburnt skin. And the legs . . . *(She kicks the legs. One side of the table collapses.)* I want you to understand this table caused me a lot of shopping around for. It comes from the very top manufacturer of ping pong tables. Examine the ball. Would I use a ball like that on a table that was no good? *(She throws him the ball.)* Go ahead. Study it all you want. The best.

MR. FESTER: Awfully impressive. *(He hands the ball back without looking at it.)*

MRS. GROAT: *(She stamps on the ball.)* What else? The painting! Directly behind you. *(She turns him about.)* An original. An investment. In two, three years, that artist will be famous. A celebrity in all the columns. I had the frame especially made up in gilt at six-twenty-five a foot, plus making. The manager in the supermarket took one look at that painting and said to me: "Confidentially, you got yourself a real buy." *(She picks some paint away with her fingernail.)* That

21

poor artist. She sits down, she paints an adorable landscape of the sea off Cape Cod. All the colors of the seasons and then some. I know my way around when it comes to art. I've been to classes. Still or moving life, nudes, daisies, trees, sunflowers, the works. I'm not joking. An original. I was planning an art gallery right here in my playroom. Genuine, original oils all over the walls. I'm a collector. Put that on your estimate.

MR. FESTER: Mrs. *(He looks at the form.)* Groat, would you prefer me to call back some time when you have less to say?

MRS. GROAT: I'm glad they sent a gentleman to interview me. You don't know a thing about ping pong, Mr. Fester, but we can't all be geniuses. I notice you're eyeing the sofa.

MR. FESTER: Are you sure?

MRS. GROAT: You gave me a look like you wanted to tell me that sofa is old. **Now** it's old. You should've seen it in its heyday. A quality sofa. An antique. It was. From my mother. I had the antique finish refinished.

MR. FESTER: The fabric seems to be badly worn.

MRS. GROAT: Waterlogged. You could put it out to sea like an ocean liner it wouldn't get this wet. Inside it's rotting away. *(She hits it with the axe handle.)* I know what you're thinking, you scoundrel: Does it open up? At the seams it opens up. That's a joke. I'm not pointing out to you what it's worth. Money isn't everything in life, Mr. Fester. Not more than eighty per cent. Eighty-five tops. That sofa came down to me from the only mother I ever had. Ask yourself if it isn't priceless. *(He gathers himself for a statement.)* Wait, Mr. Fester, don't say it smells of kerosene and ask me was I planning to burn it.

MR. FESTER: Shall we proceed with the adjustment?

MRS. GROAT: If you realized how a place like this can fill up with insects. Kerosene is deadly to bugs. Once a place's had mud all over it you can't keep them out. I had these crawlers in once before. It was the same as the horror movies, only smaller.

MR. FESTER: I am now prepared to adjust your claim.

MRS. GROAT: Make yourself cozy, Mr. Fester. Watch out for the springs and the kerosene spots. I'll run up and put us on a cup of coffee.

MR. FESTER: The company frowns if we indulge in stimulants during the working day.

MRS. GROAT: Or what would you say to something with a wallop? I have some discount bourbon. My sister swallowed half the bottle, the

22

pig. But there's enough left to give you a friendly kick in the brain. Then we'll chat. I'm a lonely, stricken woman. You're an overworked man. We have things to say to each other. I'm shy but friends tell me I'm **very** easy to get along with once you break the ice. I don't want to brag. And we'll argue about your estimate. Like people who understand what's what.

MR. FESTER: I believe you've misunderstood the company procedure. We don't argue. We adjust.

MRS. GROAT: Is that the way it is? Then let me tell you one little thing. You stint on me, you try to knife me out of full and total compensation, I'll pull a few big names out of the hat. If you think I don't have solid connections.

MR. FESTER: Mrs. Groat, allow me to clear up one matter before we go on.

MRS. GROAT: Will you wish you never started with me. You'll adjust all right. Out of court you'll adjust. I see you touching things, my **possessions,** like they had leprosy, but you don't even have the courtesy to let me explain myself. The wreckage. Like Rome. You've heard of Rome, Mr. Fester? You wait till I show you my upstairs. The steam crept up through the cork. It was hot water, remember? Into the wallpaper, over my polished furniture, the mirrors steamed up, the doorknobs rusted. Cut down your estimate on me and your people at the head office will pray for an earthquake, just for relief. *(Wagging the axe)* I took you for a gentleman and sympathetic. You had on a black tie. So you didn't play ping pong. Did I complain? Did I call you a fink or something? You want to get tough with Sugar Groat, you fink? After I've been through a damp disaster? *(She wipes her eyes with her apron and blows her nose in it.)*

MR. FESTER: Mrs. Groat, you're a young and attractive woman . . .

MRS. GROAT: You bet I am. I'm not some old chicken you can horse around with. You think you're going to get away with a buck here, a buck there, you're out of your cell. I want full and total compensation for this palace of pleasure. The whole place like it was new, and . . . *(MR. FESTER snaps his fingers and stands up majestically. She is silent. He smiles.)* You're not from the company at all.

MR. FESTER: I am. Under the old system of adjustment I might make certain recommendations as to the playroom and its deterioration.

MRS. GROAT: Just so I get what I'm asking for.

MR. FESTER: Under the new system my colleague will answer for that. I've come about the other casualty. *(She looks about the room.)* Your husband.

MRS. GROAT: Oh dear. Oh God. My poor hubby.

MR. FESTER: Where is he?

MRS. GROAT: You're too late.

MR. FESTER: What have you done with him?

MRS. GROAT: The burial was two days ago.

MR. FESTER: You moved him?

MRS. GROAT: He was lying there, right where you're standing. Face down in the mud. How was I supposed to mop up? And while I was moving him I thought: I might as well bury him.

MR. FESTER: You should know from your policy that nothing must be removed from the scene. Routine is routine.

MRS. GROAT: I didn't want trouble in my playroom. You leave a body around, before you know it the place's alive with bugs. You think I don't have pity on the dead? I can't help it. That's how I was born. Tender. Soft. Sweet.

MR. FESTER: This is quite irregular. Do you have a picture of your late husband?

MRS. GROAT: What for?

MR. FESTER: The adjustment. A full-length photograph.

MRS. GROAT: We used to play ping pong all the time. Did he have a backhand smash. He could curve a ball like a wicked message. Talk about drop shots. When we bought that table he said to me, "Sugar, if you insist on the finest, that's good enough for me." That's the kind of man he was. I wish I still had the receipt. *(She cries out.)*

MR. FESTER: I haven't asked you for a receipt.

MRS. GROAT: I had a vision of him for a second, the day we met at the racquet club on Staten Island, of which he was an exclusive member of. My girl friend introduced us, and I said, "See if you can handle this." I used to put a special chop on the ball like so: chop. He came right back with a heavy forehand drive like so: drive. After that, it was chop and drive all the way.

MR. FESTER: The photograph.

MRS. GROAT: He was so healthy before the water hit him. I couldn't stand to look at his picture again. I would die. You want color or black and white?

MR. FESTER: Just so long as it's full length and not out of focus.

MRS. GROAT: In the color I look better. *(She goes to a closet in the*

24

wall and takes out an album. They draw up chairs, sit at the table.) Watch out for this table. *(The table collapses.)* We better move to the quality sofa. *(They move.)* The first one was taken the day we arrived in Hawaii for our honeymoon. I was wearing my old blue bikini. That was years before the topless. In those days the first thing you did in Hawaii after you checked your bags was you got into a bikini. If you were a woman. I was. Some figure, no? You wouldn't imagine it looking at me in this nothing of an apron, but it's still there. I had my hair up then. You know how it is when you start your honeymoon. It gets in the way otherwise. Now, this one was in my mother's back yard, a few minutes after she passed away. I had on my new red print. You like the scoop neckline? *(She turns several pages.)* Black and white, black and white. Where's the one of me in the orange sweater? Orange or tangerine. I forget.

MR. FESTER: How tall would you say he was?

MRS. GROAT: In the new Argylls I bought him for our wedding anniversary I'd say five ten and a half.

MR. FESTER: Stand up a moment, please. *(They stand. He compares heights and checks with the photograph.)* Five ten.

MRS. GROAT: And an eighth.

MR. FESTER: We'll adjust up to that. And his weight?

MRS. GROAT: One sixty two.

MR. FESTER: Let's say one-sixty.

MRS. GROAT: You don't get away with that. He went up to one sixty five when he ate a good steak. He was broad around the stomach and those parts which you can't see properly here because his jacket is buttoned. He had the power to be a Japanese wrestler except he was pure-blooded American.

MR. FESTER: He was cruel?

MRS. GROAT: Not all the time.

MR. FESTER: Anything else you can tell me about his temperament?

MRS. GROAT: Not especially.

MR. FESTER: In view of the lack of a **corpus qui nunc est** we shall have to rely on your memory. You do remember your husband?

MRS. GROAT: Not too well. He's been gone almost a week.

MR. FESTER: Try. Try.

MRS. GROAT: *(Closing her eyes)* No good. He's blanked out. On my own I'm a helpless woman. *(Opening her eyes)* I should've had my brother-in-law here. You wouldn't find him so easy to bargain with. He's a dog. The last damp disaster I had, he comes here, he says to

25

me: *(Turning her head from side to side in a two-way conversation)*
    — You know what I'll do?
    — What will you do?
    — I'll testify I saw a man running away from the house. I tried to
stop him, I wrestled with him, he tried to stab me, he got away.
    — What's your interest in this?
    — My interest is your interest.
    — How much for you?
    — A percentage, that's how much.
    — How much of a percentage?
    — You tell me. Sixty? Seventy?
    — Why, you greedy son of a swine . . .
That's the way it would be, Mr. Fester, if I called in my brother-in-law.

MR. FESTER: *(Putting away the form)* I am sure the company can offer you an acceptable adjustment without him.

MRS. GROAT: Give me an inkling.

MR. FESTER: I'll give you an exact quotation.

MRS. GROAT: A figure?

MR. FESTER: Yes.

MRS. GROAT: What?

MR. FESTER: Not what. Who.

MRS. GROAT: Who!

MR. FESTER: I'm the adjuster.

MRS. GROAT: You're the adjustment?

MR. FESTER: You must allow for a margin of error. If I were identical to your husband I'd be your husband. You wouldn't want that.

MRS. GROAT: That I couldn't take.

MR. FESTER: I'm within half an inch of his height and a pound of his weight. If you wish to verify we can exhume the body.

MRS. GROAT: I don't like you enough.

MR. FESTER: Did you like your husband enough?

MRS. GROAT: That's my business.

MR. FESTER: I'm trying to offer you as close an adjustment as I can.

MRS. GROAT: You're not my ideal.

MR. FESTER: Take another look at your photographs.

MRS. GROAT: *(Looking)* You're right. He was a dragon.

MR. FESTER: Do you agree that I'm no worse?

MRS. GROAT: You don't play ping pong. Are you the only choice?

MR. FESTER: There's my assistant.

MRS. GROAT: Is he on a lower salary than you?

MR. FESTER: A lower everything.

MRS. GROAT: Not so good. What's he like?

MR. FESTER: A sound worker. Not as much of a dead ringer for your husband as I am. But he is younger.

MRS. GROAT: That's something. If he has an eye for a ping pong ball.

MR. FESTER: He does. One excellent eye.

MRS. GROAT: He lost an eye?

MR. FESTER: He never had more than one.

MRS. GROAT: What color is it? Blue? I love a nice blue eye.

MR. FESTER: It's hazel, verging on yellow.

MRS. GROAT: Like a squirrel's. I don't want that. I couldn't look at it.

MR. FESTER: Then it's up to me.

MRS. GROAT: What is?

MR. FESTER: You are. I'll woo you.

MRS. GROAT: How?

MR. FESTER: Manfully. *(He traps her.)*

MRS. GROAT: You wouldn't dare.

MR. FESTER: I took top honors in wooing. It's all part of the induction course. *(Seizing her)* But you're frightened of me, beautiful Belinda.

MRS. GROAT: You're so unappetizing. I don't care if I say it.

MR. FESTER: It's true. I am frightening. When I go out into the daylight the sky recedes. The sun leaps for cover. Trees bend away. The ground dissolves under my feet. Men avoid looking at me and women cringe. And yet, Belinda, while they are cringing, they are fascinated. They want me.

MRS. GROAT: With those bumps on your forehead, and that oily skin and those pointy teeth?

MR. FESTER: With them? **Because** of them.

MRS. GROAT: What are you?

MR. FESTER: Why do I fascinate women? Because the company expects me to. And I am a good company man. How could I adjust for your husband if I didn't know how to overcome you? I worked. I trained. I went beyond the training into marriage.

27

MRS. GROAT: And I thought you were an aging bachelor.

MR. FESTER: I've been married fifteen times.

MRS. GROAT: What a performer.

MR. FESTER: My third wife, Helga, will initiate you into the household. And Sharon, who is number five, will serve as your personal advisor until you find your wings.

MRS. GROAT: You're still married to them?

MR. FESTER: That's how the company grows.

MRS. GROAT: You have a harem.

MR. FESTER: You're kind to say so. I have an establishment with fireplaces in every room; you'll move into the biggest room with the widest fireplace. As the newest comer you get juniority.

MRS. GROAT: Fireplaces in every room? I can imagine the fuel bill.

MR. FESTER: Company fires are self-sustaining.

MRS. GROAT: You want me to tell the truth? I'm terrified of you. *(She tries to escape.)* I never saw such a sinister character in my life.

MR. FESTER: Thank you.

MRS. GROAT: All those other wives.

MR. FESTER: Fifteen.

MRS. GROAT: I can count. Why do you want me if you had so little satisfaction with the others?

MR. FESTER: On the contrary, I've had fifteen satisfactions in a row. Belinda, be my sixteenth satisfaction.

MRS. GROAT: Do I get to furnish my own room?

MR. FESTER: In red and black.

MRS. GROAT: I like red more than black.

MR. FESTER: We're getting someplace at last.

MRS. GROAT: Where?

MR. FESTER: To the settlement. You adjust to **me.**

MRS. GROAT: I don't think much of your technique. It stinks. You didn't even propose.

MR. FESTER: That comes next. *(Kneeling)* I love you, Belinda. I implore you to be mine and the company's. Let the world gape at our rapture. Let every blade of grass in every field stand up and gape. *(He stands up.)* Let every bush as it explodes into leaf gape. *(He approaches her.)* Let every man at his bench and every woman at her stove and every child skipping the streets with joy as his companion gape.

MRS. GROAT: What a line. *(He manipulates her on to the sofa.)*

MR. FESTER: Belinda, I am yours. Now you must be mine. The company will rejoice. *(He attacks her high and low with kisses.)*

MRS. GROAT: All I can smell on this sofa is kerosene.

MR. FESTER: There. *(Kissing her)* And there, there, there!

MRS. GROAT: I hate to think what's going to happen to this sofa frame any second.

MR. FESTER: If I said I had loved you through all eternity it would not be true . . .

MRS. GROAT: And I wouldn't believe you, believe me.

MR. FESTER: . . . But from the moment I saw that three-by-five print of you in the blue bikini I have known no peace.

MRS. GROAT: A special for George Washington's birthday. The store was open till nine. If you like that, wait till you see me in my topless. Except I would never let you.

MR. FESTER: Belinda, you are not incapable of a simple adjustment!

MRS. GROAT: Don't tell me you weigh any one-sixty-five. I'm no expert but I'd say one seventy, one seventy-two. *(He laughs and gets up.)* Look what you did to your nice black tie. What are your fifteen wives going to say when they see that?

MR. FESTER: I wore it to commemorate your late husband. It will help me to replace him.

MRS. GROAT: Replace my hubby? With a backhand smash like he had?

MR. FESTER: Belinda . . . *(He backhands a smash to her cheek.)* . . . Say you feel something for me.

MRS. GROAT: I don't like the way you adjust.

MR. FESTER: Think of the company.

MRS. GROAT: Poo on the company. Let them pay for me to go to a marriage bureau where I can choose my own adjustments.

MR. FESTER: You see, Belinda, you have a lower threshold of resistance than you thought.

MRS. GROAT: Is that so? You'll never get past me. Right this second you know what I'm doing? I'm blanking you out. I'm thinking of my hubby.

MR. FESTER: Can you see him?

MRS. GROAT: *(Her eyes closed)* Yes, now I see him. Clearly. He's in this room.

MR. FESTER: Describe him.

29

MRS. GROAT: He has on a black jacket and striped pants. Like yours. Around his neck there's a black tie. It's creased and crushed. He has sort of bumps on his forehead. He has a part in his hair like a streak of lightning. He has funny ankles. His teeth are — his teeth are — pointy. He's the image of — of — *(She opens her eyes.)*

MR. FESTER: You haven't completed the adjustment. Close your eyes again.

MRS. GROAT: No! *(She looks about desperately. She runs to the steps. He gets there first, and stands in her way. She runs toward the axe. He gets there first and puts his foot on it.)* Murder. Murder. Assassination. He's trapped me. He's going to get me. He's got me.

MR. FESTER: You're radiant. You're fiery.

MRS. GROAT: Firemen. Police. Ambulance. Blood bank. Neighbors. Sister. Brother-in-law. Preacher. Mr. President . . .

MR. FESTER: Keep at it. Come on, come on, assail me with every name and sexual image you can think of. You want to, don't you?

MRS. GROAT: Yes, oh yes.

MR. FESTER: Come on. You know them all. Out with them. And when you're done . . .

MRS. GROAT: I wouldn't say a word. I wouldn't speak. To spite you I'll slit my throat.

MR. FESTER: Nobody will hear you, thanks to the cork ceiling.

MRS. GROAT: Spare me. I'll let you get a load of me in my topless. I'll cut you in on the take, like you were my own brother-in-law. I'll give you the compensation on the lamp shade and lamp, this desirable lamp. And the plywood panelling.

MR. FESTER: I want you, Belinda.

MRS. GROAT: The sofa? My mother's own sofa with which I would never have parted with. What do you want, Mr. Fester, my soul? I don't know if I have a soul. Take the ping pong table instead.

MR. FESTER: The company is ineluctable. You will marry me.

MRS. GROAT: With my husband washed out only a few days? Is it decent? It's indecent. Let me talk to the head of your company.

MR. FESTER: The company is listening.

MRS. GROAT: You can make your company any shape you like. If my husband had been a midget — four feet two and sixty pounds — you'd have come to me like a midget.

MR. FESTER: Yes.

MRS. GROAT: There's no way out, no deal? *(He smiles.)* Help, I'm

30

THE ADJUSTMENT

dead, I'm lost.

MR. FESTER: Hush, Belinda, you're found. You've had a few days in suspension, waiting for the waters to subside, and now you are about to receive full and total compensation. Waterproof security. We are going out of here to a playroom so vast that beside it this playroom is less than a worm hole. You shall do nothing but play in the deepest, largest, most sumptuously equipped basement playroom ever constructed.

MRS. GROAT: I don't want to. I daren't . . . *(She struggles with herself.)*

MR. FESTER: Let us sing a song of degrees. *(Chanting)* I will lower mine eyes to the vaults, from whence cometh my help. My help cometh from the company which made haven and hearth. The company is thy keeper; the company is thy signature in thy right hand. The fire shall smite thee by day and the flood by night. The company shall insure thee against all discontent; it shall insure thine ease. From this time forth and even for evermore. Belinda, you are about to become my bride. *(He produces a veil, which he puts on her head, and a double brass ring, which he slips over her wrist, locking her to him.)* Let the marriage service commence, and may we play happily ever after, who are only the beginning of the beginning . . . Felicity unto us both. *(He nudges her.)*

MRS. GROAT: *(Sluggishly)* Yes.

MR. FESTER: With which I pronounce us joined in the company's name and service. And this shall be the end of the adjustment.

(MRS. GROAT goes to speak. He puts a finger to her lips and takes her arm. He begins to hum Mendelssohn's Wedding March. In time with the music they pace across the room to the foot of the steps. He nudges her. She hums with him. They walk up the steps to the door with ineffable dignity as the curtain falls.)

The Recovery

THE PATIENT
THE ACTRESS
The Old Nurse
The Young Nurse
The Patient's Wife
The Companion
THE ACTOR
The Orderly
The Engineer
The Permanent Patient
The Official

NOTE: It was the author's intention that one actress play four parts and one actor play four parts. On one occasion the play was done with separate actors for each role. It did not work as well.

THE PATIENT is lying in a hospital bed with his feet toward the auditorium. His eyelids flick open; his eyeballs swing across the sockets. He looks for the bell at his bedside, presses it. It lets out a human shriek. He starts. Nothing happens. He tries it again. It shrieks twice.

The OLD NURSE appears at the door. She is virtually blind. She taps her way into the room with a stick.

OLD NURSE: Gorgeous, gorgeous day.

PATIENT: Where?

OLD NURSE: *(She peers out the window, vertically upward.)* What a sky. Gunmetal gray. My favorite color. The sun strikes the room around this time. Any second. Now, now. Now! *(A narrow shaft of light hits the floor below the window.)* There it goes. *(The light disappears.)*

PATIENT: Nurse . . . *(She sets her sights on the foot of the bed.)* Nurse . . . *(She makes for him, studies him, shakes her head.)* Are you my nurse?

OLD NURSE: No, I'm your nurse.

PATIENT: Can you deaden that bell push?

OLD NURSE: You have a new face.

PATIENT: It's a noisy bell. It makes a human noise.

OLD NURSE: Maybe you only have new cheeks.

PATIENT: I don't like to handle an aggressive bell.

OLD NURSE: You're the heart transplant.

PATIENT: No.

OLD NURSE: *(She studies the chart at the foot of the bed.)* The elbow transplant?

PATIENT: *(Checking his elbows.)* Doesn't look like it.

OLD NURSE: You'll have a rich sunset with all those colors.

PATIENT: I look forward to it.

OLD NURSE: Don't tell me they did a cheek transplant?

PATIENT: Not any kind of transplant. I hope.

OLD NURSE: Cheeks. What next? That window too draughty for you?

PATIENT: Yes. *(She goes out. He presses the bell. She reappears.)*

OLD NURSE: I forgot to tell you. Some people say this is the finest institution of its type. Anywhere.

PATIENT: What's its type?

OLD NURSE: You're the heart transplant, that right?

PATIENT: Who knows. Let me talk to somebody who —

OLD NURSE: Stop messing with the bell push. You'll unsettle the others. Take a look at those cheeks and be humble. *(Hands him a mirror and leaves.)*

PATIENT: She's right. I have somebody else's cheeks. What are those lines? Who put parentheses around my mouth? Are they telling me my mouth is unnecessary? I'm an old man. *(Presses the bell. Pop music blares out. A MALE ORDERLY comes in with a transistor radio.)* What did I have done?

ORDERLY: What's the room number?

PATIENT: On the door.

ORDERLY: Hasn't figured out his room number yet.

PATIENT: Look on the door.

ORDERLY: *(Taking pills from a drawer)* Boy, the class of patients we get around here. Don't know their own identity. *(Bolts down a mouthful of pills.)*

PATIENT: Could you please turn the radio down? Or lower the antenna?

ORDERLY: It's for your comfort, Mac. *(Leaves it on the bedside cabinet and goes to the window.)* Goddam clouds. Rig-a-dig, rig-a-dig, ray, ray, ray. *(Dances out to the music, snapping his fingers.)*

(The PATIENT fishes painfully for the radio with his pillow. Tries to turn it off. It has no switch. Puts it under his pillow and settles back. He raises the bedclothes and looks at his body. Drops the bedclothes instantly and closes his eyes. The phone by the bed rings. He starts.)

PATIENT: Hello? Am I seven-ninety-seven? It's a fair bet. No, I'm not ready to vacate this bed. They wheeled me out of heavy surgery an hour ago. An hour ago? A century ago. Yes, most of my insides, I guess. Yes, I paid the deposit: you sent me to the bank in the ambulance before you admitted me. *(Hangs up. The OLD NURSE returns carrying a tray with metal covers over the dishes.)*

OLD NURSE: You've been looking forward to this. *(Puts the tray shakily on the bed.)* Oops. Well, it's a change to see some color to the sheets. Let's have you sitting up so you don't spill things. *(She cranks a handle at the foot of the bed. PATIENT's head and chest come up.)*

PATIENT: *(Removing a dish cover)* I couldn't wash in this. It's filthy.

OLD NURSE: Don't eat it fast. That's probably how you got your coronary in the first place.

PATIENT: *(Loudly)* I didn't have a coronary.

OLD NURSE: They all say that. We have more fast eaters in here . . . *(She goes out. The PATIENT is about to start eating. The phone rings.)*

PATIENT: Hello? Hi, Charlie. No, terrible. What sort of news? Listen, Charlie, at this moment, screw everything that went up two-and-one-eighth. Okay, electronics are ridiculously healthy; good luck to them. But Charlie, I was two hours in the recovery room. I was at the terminus. Call me back post-mortem. *(Hangs up. Opens the food covers again. Sits back, tucks the bedsheet into his neck, picks up his knife and fork. The ORDERLY comes in. With another radio.)*

ORDERLY: You started eating yet?

PATIENT: Just about to.

ORDERLY: Let me grab a handful of blood while you're fasting.

PATIENT: Would you mind taking that radio outside? *(ORDERLY leaves the radio blasting on the bedside cabinet. The PATIENT is about to reach for it; the ORDERLY seizes his arm.)*

ORDERLY: I see a juicy vein! *(He plunges a syringe into the arm.)* Jumpy, eh? *(Holds the phial of blood up to the window.)* Mm-**mm.** Just what the big boy ordered. *(Guzzles more pills.)*

PATIENT: The what boy?

ORDERLY: The vampire. The silent bloodsucker. Who else? *(Goes out. The PATIENT stuffs the new radio under his pillow. He unfastens the sheet from his neck, mops his forehead with it, tucks it in again, prepared to eat. A YOUNG NURSE enters.)*

YOUNG NURSE: No, you don't, seven-ninety-seven. While you're fasting, give me the heat and beat. *(Plants a thermometer in his mouth, takes his wrist.)* Man, that's a singing rhythm in that wrist. You a bandleader?

PATIENT: Og.

YOUNG NURSE: How was it upstairs?

PATIENT: Og og. Og og og.

YOUNG NURSE: They say he's a comical one, that big boy.

PATIENT: Og, og, og, og, og, og, og, og, og, og?

YOUNG NURSE: The size of the blade on him! And self-sharpening.

PATIENT: Og, og, og, og, og?

YOUNG NURSE: An assistant engineer told me never to refer to the blade by itself, only to the whole silent surgeon. He said it's like calling a man by his fist.

PATIENT: Og, og, og, og, og?

YOUNG NURSE: It's more personal. I'll say one thing for that silent surgeon: he goes through a fantastic amount of meat. Hey, did you foul your sheets? After I changed them just before? I didn't want you lying on the same ones as that corpse.

PATIENT: Og, og?

YOUNG NURSE: The one they hustled out ten minutes before they

35

hustled you in. *(Removing the thermometer)* Say!

PATIENT: What's up?

YOUNG NURSE: Your mercury, man. Simmer down. Now who raised your bed? You'll bust your stitches. Lethal. *(She lowers him away from the food. She looks at the food.)* That silent cook does a convincing job on the tenderloin. But you're not supposed to have imitation tenderloin. What would you digest it with? You're on the light yellow diet, imitation broth and imitation tea. Are they trying to finish you off? *(Takes the tray away from him. The ENGINEER strides in.)*

ENGINEER: Glamour puss. How's your fur? *(Pinches her. She makes a rude gesture, goes out.)* Adores me. They all do. I'm your repair-shop engineer. How's it feel, seven-ninety-seven? Pretty raw? This was a precision job. The micrometer slices to one five-hundredth of a millimeter.

PATIENT: Doctor, about the machine . . .

ENGINEER: We had a few bloops at first. All part of the game. One guy — this'll slaughter you — *(Choking up with laughter)* — arm transplant. We forgot to feed in directions for right and left installation. He had backwards hands.

PATIENT: Like this?

ENGINEER: You got it. We had to stand behind him to say how do you do. But by the time he got out of here he told me thanks. I was standing behind him. Best grip he ever had in his left hand. So let's see how you look. You were our first specimen on the automated suturing. What are you up to under those covers? Been playing the oboe? In your state? *(He pulls back the bedclothes and recoils.)* Great God!

PATIENT: Help!

ENGINEER: That's what happens sometimes.

PATIENT: It does?

ENGINEER: That part of the body turns green.

PATIENT: Green?

ENGINEER: Take it easy.

PATIENT: But green.

ENGINEER: I'm kidding. A medical joke.

PATIENT: Green . . .

ENGINEER: It's pink, I swear to God. Fresh Nova Scotia salmon, fished right out of a clean stream. Not even smoked.

PATIENT: Is green worse than pink?

ENGINEER: Not if you like green. Has your private engineer been in to see how beautifully you're doing?

PATIENT: My doctor? No.

ENGINEER: Who needs him? You're in good controls. And every time he marches in, that's another entry on your ledger. That reminds me: we had to up the charges.

PATIENT: Nobody told me.

ENGINEER: For Christ's sake, what do you expect? With the automated suturing and all! It'll be years before we recoup on the silent personnel. It's like a highway with toll booths.

PATIENT: I don't drive.

ENGINEER: Only the finest. A hopped-up telemetering system, a new data-processing deal hits the market, we snap it to bits and personalize it as only we know how. With new items you have to iron out a bug here, a bug there. But the bug that bugs you means one bug less to bug the next guy.

PATIENT: Me?

ENGINEER: It's fully neighborly. After you, the deluge. Unselfish experimentation. Cooperation. Otherwise, engineering would stop dead in its tracks. You pay your way, toll booth by toll booth, to your destination — unblemished recovery. For instance, with the new remote-vision screen, you can watch the most passionate details of the operation. From the observation room you see exactly how much blood is draining out. Everything's measured; we have full information retrieval.

PATIENT: You weren't in the operating room?

ENGINEER: During surgery? That went out with internal combustion. The silent surgeon knows how to zip through his own cycle, doesn't he?

PATIENT: I couldn't tell.

ENGINEER: It was quite a sight. And you gave some performance, seven-ninety-seven. Everybody said you were outstanding.

PATIENT: I did my best. The anaesthesia helped.

ENGINEER: You're a modest freak but you have a superb metabolism. All the graduates said so.

PATIENT: Thank you. I had an audience?

ENGINEER: Brother, their eyes were popping. Pop, pop, pop. The way you stood up to that suturing. Like I said, you were the tryout, so we threw you an extra packet of the new deadening agent. Didn't want you jiggling around in the middle of the cycle to cause a dysfunction.

37

Patients sometimes revive. They try to stand up. That leads to all sorts of dysfunctions. Not you. You lay there flat, a T-bone steak, with that mighty plunger coming down, thump, thump, thump . . .

PATIENT: Can we talk about it some other time? I have a rocky stomach. I used to get bilious in biology and have to walk away from my frog's legs.

ENGINEER: *(Shaking his hand backwards)* Keep 'em baffled. I have a date with the sexiest lobotomy you ever took in five . . . Crazy about me. Thanks forever, seven-ninety-seven. It was a thrilling and truly educational experience for the entire engineering body.

PATIENT: You're welcome . . . *(The ENGINEER goes out. The phone rings.)* Hello? Who? My doctor? No, I didn't see him around. I haven't been around. No, I have nothing to take a message **on.** *(Hangs up. The phone rings again.)* Hello? Charlie, I'm not interested. So it shot up another three-eighths. Right now I'm not buying **any** color chips. Charlie, if you knew the story here. They had machinery swarming over me. Television screens and a plunger that goes thump, thump, thump, a mighty plunger. Charlie, I was a T-bone steak . . . *(Hangs up. The phone rings again in his hand. The YOUNG NURSE returns with another tray.)*

PATIENT: Once and for all, Charlie . . . Oh, hi, dear. I just came to. Sure, I'm doing handstands and somersaults. Don't visit till next year the earliest. The young nurse is here with my lunch. Yes, she's okay-looking . . .

YOUNG NURSE: Get off that phone. Your broth'll cool off.

PATIENT: Listen, don't bring Cousin Lucy . . . She will not get a single look at my scar. *(YOUNG NURSE takes the phone from him. Hangs up.)* Thanks, nurse.

YOUNG NURSE: Nobody lets my broth get cool. *(The ORDERLY comes in.)*

ORDERLY: Lover!

YOUNG NURSE: Jerk. Take it someplace else. *(She goes out. PATIENT tries to sip the broth while on his back. ORDERLY makes a sucking noise at the retreating Young Nurse. He has a radio.)*

ORDERLY: Ta, hatcha, ta, ta. What'd you do with the tray?

PATIENT: Please may I eat my broth in peace?

ORDERLY: *(Putting radio on bedside cabinet)* Mac, when the silent people say bring a tray, I must obey and bring that tray, hatcha, hatcha, ta, ta, ta. *(Moves the broth out from under the PATIENT's spoon. Goes out, snapping the fingers of his other hand. PATIENT gets the radio under his pillow.)*

PATIENT: Somebody lift me out of this coffin. *(Rings the bell. It frightens him)* These sheets, they're making love to me. My winding sheets. The bed keeps bunking up. The walls have no tiles. I need order, confidence, lines of perspective. From a toilet seat in the lousiest hotel you've got to be in touch with tiles, within reach of a toilet tile or two, something to while away the movement. Here: not even a patch of white. This is an eyerest green room. My eyes are tired of resting. In the hallway the walls are apricot, make that peach. I could chuck up. Who needs fruit with a stomach in my condition? Maybe I'll wake up in my own bed. Or on the side of a hill, on a grassy slope under a sky. *(As he drifts off the phone rings.)* No. *(Another ring.)* Ring all you want, Charlie, let it go up ten thousand and one-eighth. *(The OLD NURSE shuffles in, fumbles her way to the phone.)*

OLD NURSE: Eh? Who? No, this is room number nine-seventy-nine. *(Hangs up.)* Who lowered my bed?

PATIENT: The young nurse.

OLD NURSE: Got no business coming in here discombobulating my room. Keep telling her she belongs in seven-ninety-seven. *(SHE raises the bed.)*

PATIENT: You'll bust my stitches.

OLD NURSE: What stitches?

PATIENT: It stitched me together after the operation.

OLD NURSE: More like welding. They have a lovely new type of rivet. And an adhesive. They don't like to call it glue. Confidentially it stinks.

PATIENT: Could you please bring me some lunch? Dinner, breakfast? Or whenever.

OLD NURSE: Yes, it's not bad as glues go. Except they say the bodily fluids make it come unstuck. *(Goes out. The PERMANENT PATIENT knocks. HE is extremely old.)*

PATIENT: Is that you, honey?

PERMANENT: I don't think so. Did the old nurse make advances to you, too?

PATIENT: I don't think so.

PERMANENT: She's married to an undertaker. She gets coffins at fifteen percent off. Without lids.

PATIENT: How much off with no bottoms? I could rest on pure earth.

39

PERMANENT: She thinks you're nine-seventy-nine.

PATIENT: What happens to the patient in nine-seventy-nine?

PERMANENT: I guess he prays.

PATIENT: He's a clergyman?

PERMANENT: God takes care of his own.

PATIENT: What do you do here?

PERMANENT: I keep things moving. Let's go. *(Pulls PATIENT's arm.)* They call me the permanent patient. Seven-ninety-three. I used to be five-sixty-two when I had migraine. I passed into middle age and collected jaundice. They promoted me to six-sixteen on the sixth floor. That threw me. I was very loyal to the fifth floor. I felt like an exile. Still one must go with the times. You coming? *(Tries to get PATIENT out of bed.)* Later I became seven-ninety-three, muscular spasms. They're not bad. Seem to keep the other afflictions away. They've settled down to one spasm every two minutes and fifty seconds. I've learned to respect my spasms.

PATIENT: Quit pulling at me.

PERMANENT: How do you like what you've got?

PATIENT: If I only knew . . .

PERMANENT: You ought to. How can you learn to respect it?

PATIENT: I'd probably be fond of it if somebody told me what it is. Other than old cheeks and a parenthesis around the mouth.

PERMANENT: Let me look. *(Tries to roll the sheets back.)*

PATIENT: I'm still in agony.

PERMANENT: We'll run on up to the solarium. All the senior patients gather there and ruminate before the big teevee shows start. They make informed guesses just by looking at you, then they vote on it.

PATIENT: I'm afraid to walk.

PERMANENT: Paraplegia.

PATIENT: I don't think so.

PERMANENT: Uremia, then, must be. Hurry. The solarium's a lot warmer since they put in the new sun.

PATIENT: Does it rise and set?

PERMANENT: Like clockwork. It stops at noon for three hours. 180 minutes of sheer overhead tan. Next winter they're installing a moon. For the insomniacs. You know, that's unfair. The rates will go up again, and what benefit do we sound sleepers get from a moon? Are you ready or do I have to haul you up ten flights to the solarium by your feet?

PATIENT: Give me peace. The peace that passeth all understatement.

PERMANENT: We're going to have a good discussion tonight about the silent suture boy. Let's get some action here.

PATIENT: *(Fighting back)* The doctor said . . .

PERMANENT: The engineer. They had their first run-through this morning with the mighty plunger on some newcomer. They didn't know what would happen.

PATIENT: What did happen?

PERMANENT: No one knows. There may be side effects. Poor dope.

PATIENT: Poor dope . . .

PERMANENT: It's still noon up there. I'm missing out on my tan. *(Tugs again. He falls to the floor.)*

PATIENT: What is it? A spasm?

PERMANENT: Bastard. You've thrown my back out of whack. Lift me.

PATIENT: I can't.

PERMANENT: Bastard. I'll get you yet. *(Crawling out)* We'll come down in a mob and get you. *(Exit. The phone rings.)*

PATIENT: Hello? They're coming to get me. No, my doctor hasn't arrived. How the hell could I put you on to him? How urgent? You thought this woman had hiccups but it turned out to be a stroke . . . Wait, I'll ring the bell. *(Rings bell; jumps.)* They're slow here. Everything's automatic. That woman must be dying of her stroke . . . *(His WIFE comes in.)*

WIFE: My tiny pet invalid. *(Smothers him, takes phone away, smooths his pillow and sheets.)* I was so worried. I almost passed out. Feel better now. Cousin Lucy stopped on the way in to talk to a friend of a friend who has very serious impetigo in semi-private room B-12 of the annex. But she's gonna see that scar if it kills you.

PATIENT: Do you have anything to eat?

WIFE: They told me not to.

PATIENT: Who did?

WIFE: Your doctor. He said I should diet if necessary.

PATIENT: Something the matter with you?

WIFE: I'm bearing up. It's been very hard without you, sweetie.

PATIENT: And you spoke to the doctor?

41

WIFE: He said it was nerves. I should relax.

PATIENT: I mean about me. What's wrong? Did you ask him? What sort of an operation did I have?

WIFE: Didn't they tell you? Well, when the patient's in danger . . .

PATIENT: What sort of danger?

WIFE: Did you enjoy the surgery?

PATIENT: The engineer said I turned green.

WIFE: That's not funny.

PATIENT: It was a joke. How about a stick of gum? A peanut?

WIFE: I'm disturbed about something else, that young nurse. I saw a **very** fetching child out there in the corridor. Is she yours?

PATIENT: Partly.

WIFE: I hope you're not getting up to mischief, honey?

PATIENT: Not even a lifesaver?

WIFE: Yes, the doctor said the strain's beginning to show, that's what it is.

PATIENT: He hasn't been in to see me.

WIFE: My veins keep standing out. And my arteries. My ankles go funny. Oo-er. *(She slumps on the bed.)*

PATIENT: You want help?

WIFE: Just let me in with you. I'll be fine if I lie down. *(Scrambles into bed.)*

PATIENT: Not in. On top.

WIFE: No good. In or nothing. *(They struggle.)*

PATIENT: If the nurse sees you . . .

WIFE: Let her walk in, the bitch. I'll put 27 inches of fingernail in her eyes. What's she trying to break up? Aren't we husbands and wives? *(Embracing him)* Sweetie, I love you in bed.

PATIENT: Take it easy. Take it away. My stitches . . .

WIFE: This is what I needed. Honey, my big one. It's been a whole week.

PATIENT: I'm out of commission. My wound . . . *(She get on top of him.)*

WIFE: I want to see it. *(She plucks at the covers.)* Now. While I'm interested. *(Another struggle. He pushes her out of the bed. On the floor)* I'll remember this. *(Gets up.)* Wait till you come to me at the end of a hard day. There are men who'd give their right hand, their leg. Only the other day — if you knew what the mechanic in the service station only offered me. Tune-ups, free winterizing, whitewall tires . . . *(She storms out. The phone rings.)*

PATIENT: God almighty, I forgot about that woman in the middle of her stroke. Hello. Yes. Did she complete the stroke yet? So it **was** hiccups . . . *(Hangs up. The ORDERLY comes in with a radio.)*

ORDERLY: Good tidings for you, seven-ninety-seven.

PATIENT: That's a blessing. Is there any way of putting a barricade in front of the door? A mob is coming down to get me. An aging mob.

ORDERLY: You don't say. Your blood sample got mixed up with someone else's.

PATIENT: Whose?

ORDERLY: Some nut with rabies. We'll try again. Hup.

PATIENT: Hup.

ORDERLY: What happened was the silent sorter gave me back the wrong needle. I never trust those silent people.

PATIENT: You certain **this** wasn't the rabies needle?

ORDERLY: Don't pester me. We can always slip you a quick inoculation. *(Holding up the phial)* Red as a rose, red as wine, red as the color of my true love's lips, red as a traffic light. Red.

PATIENT: The needle . . .

ORDERLY: Incidentally, you are still fasting?

PATIENT: Uh . . .

ORDERLY: *(Emptying several pill containers)* Keep it up. *(Puts the radio to his ear; face goes blank.)* Bee-udda-dee. Dudda-dee-doo. *(Puts the radio down.)* What's the matter? Conked out? *(He puts smelling salts under PATIENT's nose.)*

PATIENT: *(Stirring)* What?

ORDERLY: Good enough. Back among the living, like. And away we go with the red flow, down to the silent bloodsucker. *(Puts radio on bedside cabinet. Goes out. The PATIENT feebly puts the radio under his pillow. The OLD NURSE enters.)*

OLD NURSE: You the one who asked for the book?

PATIENT: No.

OLD NURSE: It's packed with color pictures. *(Cranks the bed higher.)*

PATIENT: Nurse, is rabies catching?

OLD NURSE: You'll have to check the records department. You want me to read to you?

PATIENT: What's the book?

OLD NURSE: Have it your way. *(Throws the book down and goes out.)*

PATIENT: "The Practical Mother's Guide to Home First Aid. With 200 black-and-white illustrations and 30 plates in full color." *(Opens the book, looks inside, put it down swiftly. Picks it up again, consults the index.)* Rabies, one-forty-three. Where is it? "If your child is bitten by a mad dog be sure to inform the police. If the dog belongs to you it is wise to have him put away before he bites someone else." What about the child? "Rabies can also be contracted by cats, cattle, horses and sheep, as well as goats and foxes, which should not, generally, be kept in the house." What does it **do** to you? "Rabies is characterized by tiredness, followed by trembling, followed by paralysis. Goats and sheep frequently skip the trembling stage. Without inoculation, rabies becomes fatal." *(Looking at his arm)* I'm tired and trembling at the same time. It's coming on fast. *(The phone rings.)* Hello? How's the hiccups lady? They went away? To hell with her. I've got rabies here. It's fatal without inoculation. Yes, rabies. A mad dog bit me with a needle. Paralysis. *(Rings the bell repeatedly.)* Young nurse, old nurse, come to me before I go paralyzed. I'm scared of the bell. I'm too exhausted to press the bell. But I'm trembling. I'm losing my sense of touch. I can't move. I have crumpled old cheeks. Inoculate me, somebody, save me. *(The ADMINISTRATIVE OFFICIAL enters.)*

OFFICIAL: May I come in? Actually, I am in.

PATIENT: I have rabies.

OFFICIAL: First let me check that this is seven-ninety-seven. Seventh floor, I remember that from the elevator; that part's right. We've solved the hundreds. Here's a number on the door, where it should be. Seven-ninety-seven. What a coincidence.

PATIENT: I have rabies for sure. I can feel it tearing through me.

OFFICIAL: Now the phone. Extension seven-ninety-seven. Even better. It adds up to a complete picture.

PATIENT: I'm turning paralyzed.

OFFICIAL: I'm from the administration. Pleased to meet you. I spoke to you earlier. It's about your bill.

PATIENT: I have rabies. It's fatal without an inoculation. Do you have an inoculation on you?

OFFICIAL: You've made a mistake. I'm not an engineer. I was trained as a medical technician, but I revealed an early bent for administration. Executive genius will out, no? About your deposit . . .

PATIENT: I paid it. In cash. Fresh out of the ambulance.

OFFICIAL: That's what is so strange.

PATIENT: How come?

OFFICIAL: The silent accountant should have registered something. That's the trouble with money. And then, there are unauthorized people traveling through every large institution with their hands out, so to speak. Visitors, tradesmen, even patients who flit from floor to floor. Or confidence men dressed as nurses.

PATIENT: If you think I'm going to . . .

OFFICIAL: Hush. You mustn't tremble like that.

PATIENT: I can't help it. I have rabies.

OFFICIAL: One topic at a time, seven-ninety-seven. We intend to make a checkback analysis on the silent accountant. You'll be glad to hear we have a silent investigator for this very purpose. We will make every effort on your behalf before we discard you. You said something about rabies?

PATIENT: I have it. Them.

OFFICIAL: I don't remember that on your record.

PATIENT: It isn't on my record. I just got it.

OFFICIAL: Impossible. Rabies is four-twenty-eight. *(He goes out.)*

PATIENT: *(Shouting)* I'm not about to be discarded. *(The LADY COMPANION comes in briskly.)* Do you have an inoculation?

COMPANION: *(Reaching into a shopping bag)* I have some paper airplanes. Do you like flying? Here's one that loops the loop. *(She pelts him with paper airplanes.)*

PATIENT: I have rabies and parentheses.

COMPANION: This room is an old acquaintance. I used to visit the previous patient.

PATIENT: The corpse?

COMPANION: Who?

PATIENT: I guess he wasn't when you knew him.

COMPANION: *(Launching more planes)* I'm the Companion.

PATIENT: I'm the victim.

COMPANION: I'm a volunteer.

PATIENT: I was drafted.

COMPANION: I used to be a lonely, fiftyish widow. Not now. I'm fifty-twoish and fulfilling myself. I visit all the patients I can. Forgive

45

me if I'm late some days.

PATIENT: As long as I'm alive.

COMPANION: My task is to make people feel wanted. The administration is concerned that, with all the automation, patients may think of themselves as mere numbers. What you need is somebody to pour out your heart to.

PATIENT: Mine is gummed in place. With rivets. Or else my stomach.

COMPANION: When I'm low I play chess. Do you? It's like warfare. Very cruel. All those bishops and queens. And pawns: they're the G.I.'s.

PATIENT: I was never in the war. My feet.

COMPANION: Oh how touching. I would have been a nurse but my husband wouldn't let me.

PATIENT: Jealous, maybe.

COMPANION: I don't want you thinking he was a tyrant. He's dead now. That's how I became a widow. What happened to you?

PATIENT: I was frightened by a pair of tongs. Or a tong. Forceps. No, a sole forcep. I saw no opening. I was disarmed. Down and around. If I'd seen two they, it, would at least have resembled a wishbone. But who can wish for anything from a forcep but force?

COMPANION: Well, look at the time.

PATIENT: Don't let me monopolize your airplanes. I have drooping cheeks. Also rabies. They should have quarantined me.

COMPANION: How inconsiderate. I'll make a note of that.

PATIENT: Do.

COMPANION: It's been an occasion.

PATIENT: Mine.

COMPANION: See you tomorrow?

PATIENT: Who knows?

COMPANION: Early as I can. There are many sick souls and only one me.

PATIENT: You're very healthy.

COMPANION: Life can be fun.

PATIENT: I hope you didn't catch my cheeks or rabies.

COMPANION: Haven't you been inoculated? *(He shakes his head. She flees.)*

PATIENT: I'm hungry. I'm trembling. *(Shouting)* I'm rabid. *(The*

46

ADMINISTRATIVE OFFICIAL returns.)

OFFICIAL: Our silent accountant hasn't yet located your alleged deposit, seven-ninety-seven, nor does our silent checkback analyst find any rabies on your records. Meanwhile, something else has come up.

PATIENT: What else is there? I had the wrong operation?

OFFICIAL: Yes.

PATIENT: Yes!

OFFICIAL: Nothing serious. By good fortune the surgery authorization was not processed for your signature. All it means is you underwent erroneous physical correction — but on our responsibility. It won't cost you a cent provided you sign this re-authorization voucher. This time we'll endeavor to observe standard procedure, and on your responsibility.

PATIENT: Where does that leave me?

OFFICIAL: With an extra operation at no extra charge. That's the beauty of our silent staff. All it costs us is the material expense of the additional welding. Thirty-two cents in this case. The electricity is negligible. Shall we say tomorrow morning? The silent surgeon is lying fallow between eight-o-one and eight-o-three.

PATIENT: If you think I'm about to be hacked up again by that electronic monster . . .

OFFICIAL: Please, seven-ninety-seven, we're doing our silent utmost.

PATIENT: You cut me up. You withered my cheeks. You gave me rabies.

OFFICIAL: Now, now. I'll leave the voucher here. Take as long as you want to sign it. Sleep on it. Deliberate. Thrash the matter out with yourself. I'll be back for it in ten minutes.

PATIENT: I refuse.

OFFICIAL: You don't honestly think we'd allow an experiment to leave this institution with an erroneous correction? What, and mar our records system? *(Goes out. The PATIENT slips the voucher under his pillow and lowers himself gradually from the bed. The YOUNG NURSE comes back.)*

PATIENT: Just felt like looking at this bed from the outside. And for exercise. I thought I was paralyzed.

YOUNG NURSE: Once I thought I had St. Vitus' Dance. Lean on me.

PATIENT: Nurse, you're the best leaning post I ever had. *(He stands in his nightgown. He sways and grips her shoulders.)*

47

YOUNG NURSE: Take a breath.

PATIENT: I've forgotten how. Don't move away from me.

YOUNG NURSE: What do you take me for, a murderer?

PATIENT: I feel slightly less paralyzed now. Let's walk some place. To the service elevator.

YOUNG NURSE: How about a nice climb back into bed? I'll change the sheets around you.

PATIENT: Nurse, can I ask your advice?

YOUNG NURSE: I'm only a young wheel here.

PATIENT: They're sacrificing me again to the plunger tomorrow. They want me to sign my own death warrant. That's what they mean by cooperation. Why are you laughing?

YOUNG NURSE: You know what the silent surgeon did this afternoon? Went berserk and operated on himself. Cut his own wiring to shreds.

PATIENT: Nurse, you've saved my life. But it's a machine. Don't call it "he" like it was a person. Is it really good and broken?

YOUNG NURSE: They say they'll have him fixed up by eight tomorrow morning. They just finished inventing a silent repairman who can replace the wiring in twenty seconds.

PATIENT: Nurse, the truth! Do you think I'm in shape enough to break out of here? See, I can walk easily. *(He shuffles around the bed, gripping it.)*

YOUNG NURSE: You'll have to take the bed with you.

PATIENT: Will you help me? I'll pay you any amount.

YOUNG NURSE: I'm incorruptible.

PATIENT: Don't you understand? If there's another error they'll throw me to the machine again. And again. Until I'm nothing but scar tissue. You're not listening to me.

YOUNG NURSE: I've been running all day. Just a moment. Need a little energy. *(Takes an electric cable from her pocket and plugs it into the wall. She becomes vivacious again.)*

PATIENT: Nurse, let's go. I know how you hospital workers are exploited. I'll find you a better job, a better salary. A better salary without a job. What are you up to?

YOUNG NURSE: Routine recharging.

PATIENT: Nurse, you . . . You're not a nurse. You're a silent nurse!

YOUNG NURSE: How can I be silent when I talk? No one on the staff is silent.

PATIENT: But you're not human? You don't eat food? None of you? Even the blind old nurse? Even that orderly who looks like the Mafia rolled into one? You work on batteries, on dry cells?

YOUNG NURSE: Please, we're almost self-generating.

PATIENT: But you don't have a jerky walk.

YOUNG NURSE: I hope not. I'm the latest outgrowth on the staff level: a desirable and efficient woman. I work three shifts a day, never need sleep, and everybody desires me. Everybody. You too. It's great.

PATIENT: But you run on artificial power.

YOUNG NURSE: Nowadays, what's artificial and what's natural?

PATIENT: I'm natural. I'm natural!

YOUNG NURSE: Relax, daddy-o. You'll pull out your plug. We're not permitted to furnish you an extension outlet till you're ready to bounce around.

PATIENT: Don't hand me that hogwash. *(He pats himself up and down; discovers a cord.)* Jesus, I have a tail.

YOUNG NURSE: What does it matter so long as you have your health?

PATIENT: Me! It couldn't be. Not like you, a piece of equipment . . . *(He jerks the cord out, collapses, lies motionless.)*

YOUNG NURSE: Oh my heavens, where did they put his negative terminal? In thirty seconds he's a goner. . . . They'll cut my weekend current. *(Searches up and down his body. Finds the terminal.)* Lucky you. *(Consulting her lapel watch)* In another second you'd have lost negative contact.

PATIENT: *(Coming to)* I dreamed I was a corpse.

YOUNG NURSE: Sure, sure, we all do from time to time. *(She raises the pillow to plump it. The transistor radios blare in unison. PATIENT stands up, advances.)*

PATIENT: *(Over the radios)* If - I - become - a - machine - if -I - am -then - hail - the - lord - of - machines - who - nurtures - all - with - his -blade - and - his - silence - to - him - I - yield - tomorrow - he - shall -take - me - in - his - embrace - from - eight - oh - one - to - eight - oh -three - and - I - will - know - his - love - and - pain - and - he - shall -transform - me - and - be - my - redeemer - and - my - transformer —

(The radios drown him out.)

49

The Mountain Chorus

NIGEL
DOROTHY
HACKER
SIMP
TAPPY
FONEY
LASSIE
SHEILA

From BEST SHORT PLAYS OF 1968. ed. Stanley Richards.

SCENE: *A mountaintop; the present.*
  NIGEL *enters leaning into the wind, heavily laden, wearing a climbing outfit. He unstraps a pack from his back.*

NIGEL: Dorothy, can you make it?

DOROTHY'S VOICE: I'm trying.

NIGEL: Brave girl. This looks like *it*. I'll check. *(He takes triangulation equipment from his pack and surveys the site)* Pretty near perfect. Look at that tree. Who could ask for more? On top of a mountain . . . *(He unfastens his pack. DOROTHY staggers in.)*·

DOROTHY: Finally.

NIGEL: Exactly what we hoped for. You're not too pooped?

DOROTHY: Only slightly.

NIGEL: Shall I disengage you from your pack?

DOROTHY: Bless you, Nigel.

NIGEL: Worth the climb, eh?

DOROTHY: Mm.

NIGEL: There you are. Away with the ballast. No, don't sit on your pack.

DOROTHY: I sort of folded.

NIGEL: You'll squash something. *(Lays a handkerchief on the ground for her.)* How's that?

DOROTHY: Homey.

NIGEL: Happy birthday.

DOROTHY: Thank you. Coming here was sheer inspiration.

NIGEL: I can't take all the credit.

DOROTHY: Thank you.

NIGEL: Fine place to revive the old bliss.

DOROTHY: Oh, Nigel.

NIGEL: And a tree to ourselves. A darn good tree. Pine, maybe.

DOROTHY: Gorgeous.

NIGEL: Sort of a windbreak, too. Bring the binocs?

DOROTHY: In your pack.

NIGEL: No, yours.

DOROTHY: Excuse me, Nigel.

NIGEL: You didn't forget them?

DOROTHY: Wasn't my responsibility.

NIGEL: Let's not bicker about responsibilities.

DOROTHY: Please, Nigel. On my birthday.

NIGEL: Well, dammit, we need the binocs. How will we know we're alone?

51

DOROTHY: Here they are. In my pack.

NIGEL: Ha. *(He takes them from her.)*

DOROTHY: Nigel.

NIGEL: What are you worried about now?

DOROTHY: Love me?

NIGEL: Love you. And me?

DOROTHY: You too. Yes, much.

NIGEL: *(Using the binoculars)* Well and truly alone. All those other mountains. But miles away. Swarming with tourists. Wanted to make sure. Now I'll see to the tent.

DOROTHY: Will it be out of sight of the other mountains?

NIGEL: In the hollow here. *(He begins to erect the tent.)*

DOROTHY: But from the air? Planes and so forth?

NIGEL: Sturdy fabric. Very opaque. I asked the salesman.

DOROTHY: Don't you want a drink first?

NIGEL: Later.

DOROTHY: Even a little one?

NIGEL: I said later.

DOROTHY: Nigel.

NIGEL: What now?

DOROTHY: Love me?

NIGEL: Love you.

DOROTHY: And . . . ?

NIGEL: And me?

DOROTHY: You, too.

NIGEL: Damn awkward with this wind.

DOROTHY: Can I help?

NIGEL: No. It's your birthday.

DOROTHY: It's a pretty tent.

NIGEL: If you say so.

DOROTHY: Expensive?

NIGEL: Nothing's too expensive for your birthday.

DOROTHY: Thank you.

NIGEL: Blast this wind. And the ground is solid rock. How do they expect you to put up a tent in a place like this?

DOROTHY: Leave it till later.

NIGEL: I will not. Tent's the first thing we need. If a tree can stand here, so can a tent.

DOROTHY: Unroll the mattresses?

NIGEL: If you like.

DOROTHY: I brought the blue sheets with the pattern. Not the white ones. And the blue pillowcases.

NIGEL: Why the blue?

DOROTHY: Matches the top of the mountain.

NIGEL: There it is. Our tent.

DOROTHY: Stunning.

NIGEL: Oh . . .

DOROTHY: Nigel, what is it?

NIGEL: Should've made up the beds first. How are we going to fix them inside that dinky little tent?

DOROTHY: I'll do it.

NIGEL: You'll knock the tent over.

DOROTHY: No, I'm careful with tents.

NIGEL: Forget it. *(He takes the mattresses and slides them into the tent.)*

DOROTHY: I'll be fixing the drinks.

NIGEL: My job.

DOROTHY: I want to be useful.

NIGEL: Chill the glasses.

DOROTHY: Where's the insulated bag?

NIGEL: Your pack. Top left compartment.

DOROTHY: Do we have enough ice?

NIGEL: We're strong on cubes. Not sure about the crushed. *(Pause)* The beds just about fit.

DOROTHY: Goody.

NIGEL: Which way up do our heads go? If we put them next to the entrance flap we'll catch a draught. If we have them at the other end, how will we ever get in?

DOROTHY: I'm for lots of breeze. These winds stimulate me. Glass chilled enough?

NIGEL: Next to my cheek, please.

DOROTHY: Yes?

NIGEL: Could be a mite cooler. There are the beds. Not the most

53

thrilling bedmaking job I've ever seen, but sleepable.

DOROTHY: Nigel, they're darling.

NIGEL: Now for the rug. *(He spreads it out in front of the tent.)*

DOROTHY: Nigel, a white fur rug.

NIGEL: For the you know, preliminaries.

DOROTHY: How considerate. Where did you get it?

NIGEL: Sporting goods store.

DOROTHY: Real fur?

NIGEL: Imitation polar bear. Washable. Static-free.

DOROTHY: It's all gruff and grumpy. I love it.

NIGEL: What next? The banner.

DOROTHY: Yes, please. Nigel, why don't we . . . ?

NIGEL: What?

DOROTHY: Put it on the tree?

NIGEL: Let me think. Yes, the tree would work. *(He takes out a college banner and nails it to the tree.)*

DOROTHY: The tree suits it.

NIGEL: What about the suntan oil?

DOROTHY: I brought lotion. Didn't want to grease up the sheets. But Nigel, you're not sunbathing in this wind?

NIGEL: Might get a windburn.

DOROTHY: A good point.

NIGEL: On the other hand, the sun may come out later. Time for refreshments. What're you having?

DOROTHY: What are you?

NIGEL: Vodka martini.

DOROTHY: Japalac, please.

NIGEL: One dash of raspberry syrup? Have two. It's your birthday.

DOROTHY: One and a half. Light on the rye.

NIGEL: *(Mixing)* How are the glasses coming along?

DOROTHY: Try.

NIGEL: Good. Keep them at that temperature.

DOROTHY: *(Looking through the binoculars)* Astounding view. In every direction.

NIGEL: Very varied.

DOROTHY: Hors d'oeuvres. Caviar or whitefish dip?

NIGEL: A nibble of both.

DOROTHY: On an onion biscuit?

NIGEL: Why not?

DOROTHY: I'll risk the health pumpernickel.

NIGEL: Where's the tray? *(She gives him a silver tray. He arranges the drinks and the hors d'oeuvres. He sets up stack tables and unfolds a pair of chairs. They put their drinks on coasters.)*

DOROTHY: Whose toast?

NIGEL: It's your birthday.

DOROTHY: That's hard. I'm thinking. Got it. To **everything**.

NIGEL: I'll drink to that. *(He does.)*

DOROTHY: The Japalac is overpoweringly good.

NIGEL: The raspberry syrup. I put in one and three quarters.

DOROTHY: Nigel, you shouldn't've.

NIGEL: The caviar isn't bad.

DOROTHY: Nor is the whitefish.

NIGEL: Another toast?

DOROTHY: Interesting idea. Your turn.

NIGEL: To a successful conclusion.

DOROTHY: Nigel, you're so risqué.

NIGEL: Oh.

DOROTHY: What?

NIGEL: A mark on the silverware.

DOROTHY: Tarnish?

NIGEL: Looks like it.

DOROTHY: Borrow mine.

NIGEL: It doesn't matter.

DOROTHY: Not quite hygienic. But my lipstick has practically worn off.

NIGEL: I said it doesn't matter.

DOROTHY: Nigel.

NIGEL: Yes?

DOROTHY: Love me?

NIGEL: Love you.

DOROTHY: You forgot again.

NIGEL: And me?

DOROTHY: You too. Nigel, this is heaven.

NIGEL: Thank you. Must keep up with the sexual revolution.

DOROTHY: The what?

NIGEL: You know, the younger generation.

DOROTHY: It's better than our honeymoon.

NIGEL: Higher up, anyway.

DOROTHY: Remember that Bermuda beach hut where you . . . ?

NIGEL: I could really wear swim shorts.

DOROTHY: Nigel, you're awfully well preserved.

NIGEL: Thank you. I'll get out the transformer.

DOROTHY: Nigel, shouldn't we . . . ?

NIGEL: What?

DOROTHY: Be at it.

DOROTHY: Must get in the mood first. Radio or TV?

DOROTHY: TV, please. More to look at. *(He takes out a portable set and twiddles.)* Oh, dear. Nothing but soap opera.

NIGEL: We'll try the stereo.

DOROTHY: No, leave this on. Something to look at.

NIGEL: Contrast is only so-so. Brightness not much better.

DOROTHY: One of those other mountains getting in the way?

NIGEL: Impossible. This is a mountaintop model.

DOROTHY: They think of everything.

NIGEL: For a price.

DOROTHY: Can you up the sound?

NIGEL: On full already. Better hook up the stereo. We ought to get plenty of dimensional resonance with the valley down there, the sky up there.

DOROTHY: There's a beautiful cloud.

NIGEL: Don't see it.

DOROTHY: Behind the TV antenna.

NIGEL: Nasty-looking fellow.

DOROTHY: Has a head like a unicorn. Would you refresh my Japalac?

NIGEL: Must clear up this wiring first. You got the leads from the preamp tangled in your pack with the audio cable. *(DOROTHY helps herself to another drink.)*

DOROTHY: That unicorn. It has two horns.

NIGEL: If the transformer's not in shape, we're sunk. I wouldn't be surprised if the connections took a hell of a jolting up that hill.

DOROTHY: Not two horns. Three. And three heads. Four, five, six, seven . . . Believe it or not.

NIGEL: For God's sake, Dorothy. Don't keep on with your horns while I'm concentrating.

DOROTHY: The next mountain on the right has a peach of a waterfall. Most exhilarating to watch. All that foam. Bunching up at the edge. Then — whoosh. Nigel, what would happen if this mountain turned into a volcano? Right underneath us? Would we be swallowed up? In boiling lava?

NIGEL: No.

DOROTHY: Why not?

NIGEL: This isn't volcano country.

DOROTHY: How can you be sure?

NIGEL: I found the red terminal.

DOROTHY: I'm having another Japalac. Nigel!

NIGEL: Go ahead. It's your birthday.

DOROTHY: I'm putting in three raspberry syrups and two ryes.

NIGEL: Where's the outlet for the black terminal? That's all I ask.

DOROTHY: Come and sit down. You're all tense on my birthday.

NIGEL: So. Now we'll see if the whole thing goes up in smoke.

DOROTHY: That would be a shame. Personally I couldn't care less.

NIGEL: Hear that? *(Violinny dance music begins.)* Reception's terrific. I'll move the other speaker three or four inches.

DOROTHY: Have another vodka martini.

NIGEL: Are you hearing balanced sound?

DOROTHY: I'll say. Sit on the polar bear rug.

NIGEL: Give me a couple of minutes. To unlax.

DOROTHY: Put your head in my lap.

NIGEL: I won't be able to see the screen.

DOROTHY: Turn it. *(He does, then sits in the folding chair. She tries to take his head in her lap.)*

NIGEL: Don't think much of the color. The folding chair is folding under me.

DOROTHY: How about this? *(She lies on the white rug.)*

NIGEL: Be over before long. Pity. For soap opera this is quite respectable.

DOROTHY: The unicorn cloud's gone. Surged away. Here comes its baby.

NIGEL: Unicorns are out in force today. What's happening to the stereo? The automatic frequency control must have slipped to manual. Dorothy, we're skidding between stations.

DOROTHY: It does sound weird. To hell with it.

NIGEL: And the tuner's new. Paid on the spot for it. The check's gone through by now. Should have taken out a charge account there.

DOROTHY: I think it's another radio. Somebody else coming.

NIGEL: Christ! I made sure we'd have this peak to ourselves.

DOROTHY: Snub them bitterly. Keep watching the TV. *(She gets up and joins him.)*

NIGEL: Why should they enjoy the privileges of our TV and stereo? Who lugged them all the way up —? *(NIGEL switches off the radio, turns down the television sound.)* Here's a book. Read.

DOROTHY: I'm off books lately. No ads or anything.

NIGEL: The New Yorker?

DOROTHY: That's more like it. Lots of color. Nigel, they couldn't have chosen a worse time to invade us. I was getting receptive. Tell them it's my birthday. If they take the hint.

NIGEL: Won't be for long. We'll freeze them out. *(The other radio approaches. Six young people appear. Four are boys: HACKER, TAPPY, SIMP, FONEY. Two are girls: SHEILA, LASSIE.)*

HACKER: By the tree. *(To NIGEL)* Hi, Pops. *(To the others)* In a clean, gentleman-type circle.

TAPPY: Is this for a war council?

HACKER: Don't get brighty with me. *(Hits TAPPY in the face.)*

TAPPY: What did I say?

HACKER: *(To SIMP, who has the radio)* And cut that radio.

SIMP: I could make it like low.

HACKER: I said cut it. *(Throws the radio over the edge.)* A nice drop. Must be six, seven hundred feet down. Made sweet music all the way.

SIMP: But Hacker . . .

HACKER: I told you you wasn't to bring it. Take the roll call.

SIMP: My brother bought that radio.

HACKER: Take the roll call or your brother will have to buy a new brother. *(LASSIE leans against the tree and decorates her eyes with a green pencil. FONEY necks with SHEILA.)* Foney, get off that chick's chest while we're taking our roll call.

DOROTHY: Are they planning to stay here?

NIGEL: If they are I'll have a stern word with them.

HACKER: Say, Pops, you don't have to breeze or nothing. Stick around with the broad.

NIGEL: This lady is my wife.

HACKER: Nice going, Pops. Simp, did I hear you not reading the roll call?

SIMP: Hacker, honorary president.

HACKER: Here.

SIMP: Simp, honorary secretary. Here. Foney, honorary treasurer.

FONEY: What? Here.

HACKER: I told you: stop chewing at that chick.

SIMP: Tappy, honorary advisory observer.

TAPPY: Here. What's all this about?

HACKER: Ask me one more question. Just one more. Okay, Mr. Secretary. Take the minutes of the last meeting.

(NIGEL stands up)

NIGEL: Pardon me. My wife and I purposely chose this isolated peak.

SIMP: This what?

HACKER: You stiff. Keep your ears ungummed. The man said, "Peak." That right, Pops: Peak?

NIGEL: And if you intend to remain here . . .

HACKER: We intend, Pops. But that don't give you no reason to blow. Is somebody hustling you? Simp, why did you quit reading?

SIMP: "The exec committee met . . . "

SHEILA: Haw.

SIMP: Shut your goddam lip.

SHEILA: Go stuff.

SIMP: Hacker, shall I give it to her?

HACKER: Mr. Secretary, I didn't like that word "goddam." That is not a gentleman-type word. Get going with the minutes.

SIMP: I keep thinking about that sonofabitching radio.

HACKER: Any more slang like that out of you while we got company and I'll take your face apart.

SIMP: "The exec committee met in conclave at the corner table in Kuppenheimer's Drugstore & Paperback Jamboree. Present were the following Toreadors . . . "

SHEILA: Haw.

HACKER: Give it to her.

SIMP: Me?

HACKER: You. Anybody. Everybody. *(The boys all strike SHEILA.)*

LASSIE: You scum. Hitting a girl. What you want to do that for?

HACKER: That's not my idea of a quality-type word. Scum. Give it to her. *(They strike LASSIE. She sits and weeps, the green running down her face.)*

SHEILA: Foney, after that, don't you never come near me again.

FONEY: It was a little hit, baby. Here, I'll make it better.

NIGEL: I don't wish to intrude on your deliberations. I must remind you, though, that first claims come first. I expect you to honor ours.

HACKER: Sure, Pops. You sit back and make like you're in your own mansion. Simp?

SIMP: "Present were the following Toreadors from the exec committee: Hacker, Simp, Foney. Also, Lassie, Sheila and Tappy, observers . . . " Ahh . . .

NIGEL: And I don't approve of your striking girls.

HACKER: Anything you say, Pops. Simp, if you quit reading them minutes one more time you'll get my toe where you can't wear it.

SIMP: "The exec committee agreed with the honorary president that the proposed rumble between the Toreadors and their deadly foes, the Muckrakers, will, shall, and should take place as heretofore decided by the honorary president. The meeting thereupon ended."

HACKER: Who put in that word "deadly"?

SIMP: Me, I guess.

HACKER: Is that a gentleman-type word?

SIMP: I'll take it out.

HACKER: Gink. You delete it.

NIGEL: Are you ignoring my request? Perhaps I should warn you that I can enforce it. As a former fullback who has maintained his condition by climbing and other activities —

HACKER: Does everybody accept the minutes? Minutes accepted.

NIGEL: And further, as an amateur boxer of no mean prowess —

HACKER: Pops, you're the champ. So we Toreadors have to make up our executive mind why said rumble didn't take place.

FONEY: Somebody ratted.

NIGEL: Threats don't seem to deter them. Should I take action?

DOROTHY: Nigel, they're young.

TAPPY: Look, is this a war council?

HACKER: Give it to him. *(The boys descend on TAPPY and strike him.)* One warning ought to be enough, Tappy. Now, like Foney explained, **somebody** ratted. Except ratted is not a quality-type word. Somebody **betrayed**. Some canary flew to the boys in blue and said, "The Toreadors figure to rumble." And the blue boys greased him up good. He took away all the green he could handle.

TAPPY: Don't we have no idea who done it?

HACKER: We have a very fine idea.

TAPPY: Then what?

HACKER: Then we're holding an official-type inquiry.

FONEY: Great!

HACKER: Shut your ugly-type yap.

FONEY: Maybe I want to confess.

HACKER: Yes — ?

FONEY: . . . I was kidding.

HACKER: At an inquiry? *(Striking him.)* Do I have to keep all the order around here with my two single hands?

SHEILA: What you want to hit him for?

FONEY: Now you give me a black eye or something.

HACKER: We better level that off. *(Strikes him in the other eye.)* We don't want our treasurer losing his honorary balance.

LASSIE: He lost it when he come out of his mother's whatever he come out of.

HACKER: Lassie, one more squawk and I'll hand you the straight treatment. I'm still waiting for this confession. It better fly out quick. And it better be a clean in language Toreador-type confession all the way.

NIGEL: This is intolerable.

DOROTHY: Nigel, let's move on.

NIGEL: Uproot the tent? Set up the stereo again after it's going so beautifully? I give them five minutes. After that, I boot them off this peak.

DOROTHY: They've taken over.

HACKER: *(His eyes fixed on SIMP)* Who's about to confess?

61

SIMP: *(Squirming)* I don't have nothing to confess. Except if I confess on somebody else.

HACKER: You want to sing a song — ? Point a finger? . . . That's a bad sign.

SIMP: If the guilty one don't confess I mean I'll confess on him.

HACKER: What you say to that, Foney?

FONEY: Me? It's not true.

HACKER: You never spoke to no blue boys?

FONEY: I was a gentleman-type Toreador all the way through.

HACKER: Get your hand outa her skirt when you tell me that.

FONEY: I swear on my mother's coffin.

HACKER: Your mother is alive and living.

FONEY: She's got to go into a coffin some day, don't she?

HACKER: How about Tappy there?

TAPPY: You picking on me again?

HACKER: Don't throw me a question when I throw you a question.

TAPPY: How **about** me? And how about **you**, Hacker?

HACKER: After I warned you. You threw me two questions. I'm going to push your mouth where it ought to go, down your ignorant-type throat.

NIGEL: Four minutes up.

DOROTHY: Nigel, before you explode give them fair warning. Listen to me, you boys. How long are you staying here with these games?

HACKER: Games, lady? If this is games I like to know what's for real. Right, Pops?

NIGEL: Do you minds not calling me "Pops." I'm old enough to be your father.

FONEY: How old would that be, Pops? You must be damn near thirty.

HACKER: Foney, apologize to the old folks for that word you said there. Or I'll rub your nose on that tree till one of them wears out.

FONEY: I apologize.

HACKER: *(Turns back to NIGEL.)* Like I said, Pops, you can sit around.

NIGEL: I mean to, I assure you.

DOROTHY: How did you get up here?

SIMP: We come in the convertible.

NIGEL: I suggest you scramble back into your convertible and take off instantly.

DOROTHY: A road. Nigel, we may get crowded off this mountain by more hooligans. Let's pack.

HACKER: Stick around, Pops. You might see something you can tell the world.

NIGEL: Be sensible, Dorothy. We can't unmake the beds in front of these snickering infants.

HACKER: It's a straight invitation. You wouldn't want to reject me, would you, Pops?

DOROTHY: How long will you be here?

HACKER: You know how it is, lady. When you have something on your executive mind. What you do, Pops? You a lawyer? Our defendant could sure use a hot lawyer. It might shorten this inquiry up.

TAPPY: What you mean, defendant, Hacker?

HACKER: You been in plenty big law cases, Pops? The newspaper-type kind of cases?

NIGEL: I am not a lawyer.

HACKER: Okay, Pops, you're the like citizen-type.

NIGEL: Will you please refrain from calling me "Pops"?

HACKER: Refrain?

NIGEL: Yes. Desist.

HACKER: Desist, refrain, desist. Did you clunks hear them dignity-type words? Simp, you better took them down in your minutes.

SIMP: Just wrote them, Hacker.

HACKER: Pops, you certainly are the class we need around here.

DOROTHY: Nigel, don't let them provoke you . . .

HACKER: Look at it this way, Pops. Nobody's hanging on to you by the short hairs or nothing. You want to breeze —

NIGEL: By God, Dorothy, just step out of sight and I'll . . .

HACKER: Nothing is going to like happen, Pops. Be our guest.

NIGEL: We were here first.

HACKER: Sure you was. *(Turns, ominously.)* So, we come back to Tappy . . . *(TAPPY starts to dash away. HACKER dives at his legs and brings him down, then sits on his head.)* You slobs see how slowball you are around here? If I wasn't on the team everybody would like cut out. Now. What's with Tappy? He afraid of this legal-type inquiry? Maybe he's sorry he ratted on his colleague-type buddies.

TAPPY: I didn't do nothing. You're breaking my neck.

HACKER: Tap, take it easy. All that bouncing makes me not comfortable.

NIGEL: You have no right to squash that boy's head.

HACKER: Cool it, Pops. Let's not get all busy before we investigate what this inquiry is going to prove.

TAPPY: You're killing my neck.

NIGEL: Let the boy rise and speak for himself.

HACKER: You hear that, Tappy? You got yourself a lawyer. One of the biggest. Pops here is the king of the brighty lawyers.

SIMP: Let's swing. I'm getting the chills. *(He idly punches FONEY's arm. FONEY comes out of his necking trance with SHEILA, and punches back. They beat away at each other's biceps. HACKER gets off TAPPY's head and pulls him to his feet by the collar.)*

HACKER: Okay, let the inquiry roll.

NIGEL: Release that boy.

TAPPY: I didn't squeal. Not one word.

HACKER: You'll squeal plenty before this deal is through. Okay, you gentlemen of the jury. Unsuck your face from that cheap-type broad. This is big business for we Toreadors. Let's have respect for the law. Go ahead, Tappy. Spill.

NIGEL: Release him. I shan't say it again.

TAPPY: What you going to do to me?

HACKER: Now, Tappy, could I tell you that before I knew if you was like one thousand per cent guilty or less?

TAPPY: I mean, if I was to confess on myself, would I get a reprieve-type sentence?

HACKER: What you think this jury is for? Making bargains with a prisoner? Either you confess or . . .

TAPPY: Mister, will you protect me?

NIGEL: Before I say another thing, my boy, I want you to understand that whatever you've done or have not done is hardly my concern.

DOROTHY: *(Apprehensively)* Nigel! Beds, banner, tent, everything . . . Come!

NIGEL: *(To TAPPY)* I don't envy you your fate but perhaps this incident will teach you to select thoughtful companions, not roughnecks.

HACKER: Hey, Pops, watch out for the foul-type language. Like we can lose our cool, too.

TAPPY: Crud on the lotta you. So I betrayed! You was always coming down on me. I was the youngest nobody around. Now I count. I went to the cops. I cut that rumble dead. I was on the both sides at the same time. All the world trusted me. That was pretty good, hey?

HACKER: Everybody's friend. A very sweet-type arrangement.

TAPPY: You bet your butt it was. *(NIGEL steps forward. DOROTHY clutches at him.)*

HACKER: And no fuzz didn't hand you no bread? No crumbs . . . ?

TAPPY: No.

FONEY: Clobber the truth out of his guts.

SIMP: I knew it was him all along.

HACKER: You see what these Toreadors are asking for, Tappy? They want a bit of your like blood. Keep them unhappy. Spit up the truth.

TAPPY: I am.

HACKER: Fix him against the tree. For a total confession. *(FONEY and SIMP pin TAPPY against the tree.)* And here we have a rock with kind of edges. *(He presses the edge into the small of TAPPY's back. TAPPY cries out, painfully.)* Tappy, what's all the yelling? We didn't even start yet . . . A bit of friendly pressure. Until we come to the full truth.

TAPPY: *(Relenting)* Okay. Okay. All the getting cut up and beat up all the time . . .

HACKER: *(Ignoring TAPPY's attempted explanation)* . . . Not only did you rat. You lost your respect for the decent things in life. It don't twist your insides when the Muckrakers cross up our honor?

TAPPY: Get that rock thing outa my back.

HACKER: You was afraid you might be the somebody got hurt in the rumble.

TAPPY: Not only me. *(More pained)* That rock . . .

NIGEL: Dorothy, I don't want to push you aside, but . . .

HACKER: We Toreadors wouldn't destroy a colleague's backbone. Get that rope and tie him a very fine noose.

NIGEL: That's my mountain rope.

HACKER: We pay you for it, Pops.

NIGEL: To lynch him with?

HACKER: No question of a lynch. We just tie him to this strong-type tree and let him dangle his yelling tail. We wouldn't damage him. He's an associate. Except he ratted. He'll be safe as home hanging over this nature-type cliff.

TAPPY: How come it's always my buddies get cut up? Beaten? Never one of you exec committee guys for a change? The whistle blows, you're out there in back of us.

HACKER: Hear that, Pops? That's the type criminal mind you're facing here. I mean, **mean**.

NIGEL: Let that boy go! *(He pushes DOROTHY aside, strides over to FONEY and SIMP, and pulls their arms away. TAPPY darts behind the tree and escapes.)*

HACKER: *(Stalkingly)* Why'd you want to do a thing like that, Pops — ? *(He leaps at NIGEL and knocks him to the ground. FONEY and SIMP join in. DOROTHY screams. After a struggle, the boys tie NIGEL with the rope.)* Pops, you're mean, like Tappy. Letting him cut out. It could waste a whole 'nother day before we capture him. We thought you was more polite . . .

DOROTHY: Take your hands off him!

HACKER: We don't use our hands, lady. This like rope does it all.

DOROTHY: It's my birthday.

HACKER: All the very best, lady, from all of us on the exec committee.

DOROTHY: You degraded young ruffians, you animals, you shit!

HACKER: I could of swore you was a gentleman-type lady. And here you bust out with them kind of personal statements.

NIGEL: You're not to lay a hand on her, you hear?

HACKER: What's all this about hands? *(Holds out his hands.)* Here's my hands, Pops. Not fooling with a thing. You're just too heated, Pops. *(He ties the other end of the rope to the tree.)* We'll just hang you out in that fresh air.

DOROTHY: He's done nothing to you!

HACKER: . . . Only let our defendant cut out. Only broke up our proceedings. But we don't got a thing against old Pops. . . . You interested in space, Pops?

NIGEL: Whatever you do, let my wife go! She's a woman . . .

HACKER: Oh, I seen that, Pops, all the way up and down. You know? Like my personal mother is a woman. A very refined woman. You refrain and desist, Pops. And just don't rock the rope.

66

NIGEL: If you touch her — !

HACKER: Shame on your snazzy head, Pops, for thinking such-type things. This isn't my age of pickle. Okay, let him sink. *(FONEY and SIMP lower NIGEL over the edge. DOROTHY rushes toward him. HACKER places himself in her way. He steps forward. DOROTHY sinks down onto the ground silently, just staring blankly ahead. NIGEL's voice is heard, but not his words.)*

SHEILA: Anybody would think they was feebs the way it takes the both of them to lower one poor schnook who isn't no bigger than either one of them put together.

LASSIE: Some musclemen.

SIMP: *(Straining)* I'll talk to you later, you hairy hooker. *(He and FONEY finish letting the rope out. They stand back.)*

FONEY: It's a powerful-type rope.

SIMP: A cinch.

FONEY: Hold forever. *(The tree suddenly comes out of the ground and topples over the edge after NIGEL.)*

LASSIE: You Toreadors forget about the thin soil around here? *(DOROTHY looks up, sees that the tree is missing, screams, and goes back into her stupor.)*

FONEY: It was this wind must have done it.

LASSIE: You geek-type murderers! Poor old guy . . .

SHEILA: He wasn't so old . . .

FONEY: *(Approaching DOROTHY)* Lady, it was a accident. Right, Hacker?

HACKER: That's right, lady. The boys didn't mean a thing.

FONEY: What you mean . . . **the boys?**

HACKER: *(Ignoring him)* Listen, lady, a deal. We wouldn't let you carry him home alone in that wet state. We was like attached to old Pops. We'll bring him up here. And, if they ask you, we was the witness. We saw, see? The whole mess . . .

FONEY: Boy!

SIMP: Boy, ahoy! Wow!

FONEY: This looks like **it!**

HACKER: Quit the brighty talk! You two slobs was the one tied the knots. First, we got to bring back old smashed-up Pops. Don't move a toe, lady. We'll be up here again in one second flat, so you don't have to be without old Pops on your birthday. *(They look back at*

DOROTHY. *Then they run. There is the sound of their car racing away. After a moment, DOROTHY rises and slowly crosses back to the encampment.)*

DOROTHY: All this sun. So cold. Must be . . . late . . . *(Then, suddenly)* Nigel! **Nigel!** *(Weeping)* And the banner. Your forlorn banner . . . *(After taking a long drink and finishing NIGEL's, she notices the television set which is still on. She crosses to her chair and sits down, staring blankly and sobbing. Gradually, the television begins to interest her.)* Can't hear a thing . . . *(She turns up the volume. She continues to sob now and again. The television program takes hold of her. She stares at it, intently. Her sobs diminish. She smiles. She laughs. . .)*

Curtain

The Imp or Imps
one act of mixed medicine and some music

CASSIO, doctor
FELICITY, receptionist
ARTHUR, surgeon
GARNISH, copywriter
HARLOTTA, unmothered wife
CHORUS, unseen

FELICITY is at her desk in the reception alcove between Cassio's consultation room and a waiting room. The door of the waiting room bulges from time to time. Patients cough, groan, whine, clap, and rhythmically stamp.

SONG   FELICITY: *(Singing)* Take good care of your hide
And what's left of your pride
Protect your left side with your knee
Tell yourself: My health depends on me.
(Recitative) Kneel, don't stand on your neighbors' shoulders.
Make it comfortable for the neighbors on your shoulders.
Everybody has to live, unfortunately. Lay off the stamping:
you're killing the folks one layer below you.
(Singing) Have respect for your soul
Any your ultimate goal
And the whole of your life to be
Tell yourself: My health depends on me.

69

(Pushing a phone button) Doctor's office. A splinter? Your second in a week? It's the season, everybody's getting em, the weather's so strange. Come on in for a complete checkup: one o'clock. *(Another button)* Doctor's office. Nicked yourself shaving? But it really **hurts**. Come on in for a decisive checkup: one o'clock. No, there's no waiting. *(Another button)* Doctor's office. A blackhead? That's awful. On her **back**? Wow. I know: you're afraid she'll be permanently disfigured. Bring her in: one o'clock, yes, for a checkup and probe, with X-ray, diathermy, and javelins. And tell her to quit picking at it. *(Another button)* Doctor's office. Typhoid, did you say? How do you know? Yep, that sounds like it. Come on in, bring the infected family, all of them. Your contagious party reservation is for one o'clock, including explorative checkups . . . . *(The noise swells out from the waiting room.)* No use hammering. Door never opens before one. The doctor has commitments. I expect him for sure this week. *(Another button)* Doctor's office. A sore elbow? *(Another button)* Doctor's office. Thin hair? *(Another button)* Doctor's office. Purple tonsils? *(Another button)* Doctor's office. Shrunken bladder? Doctor's . . . *(CASSIO enters through a side door. FELICITY hangs up. Phone lights keep flashing.)*

SONG   CASSIO: Hello, nurse.

      FELICITY: Hello, doctor

      CASSIO: How's the crowd?

      FELICITY: Big as ever.

      CASSIO: Rowdy? Loud?

      FELICITY: You'll win em over
Genius, you always do.

      CASSIO: I love my receptionist.

      FELICITY: I love my doctor boss.

      CASSIO: We go together

      FELICITY: Like a cowboy and his hoss.

CASSIO: Felicity!

FELICITY: Cassio! *(They kiss hungrily.)* Seducer.

CASSIO: Kitten, witch, putain. *(They kiss again.)*

FELICITY: We need more barbed wire the other side of that door.

CASSIO: Expenses, expenses.

FELICITY: Good game this morning?

CASSIO: Tiring.

FELICITY: Overnight rain on the course?

CASSIO: A moist and treacherous green.

FELICITY: My favorite color.

CASSIO: My antagonist was hitting a wicked ball. But my wrists were unbeatable. I nosed ahead on the first nine with a sensitive thirty-seven. We mashied to a standstill for the last hole. I'm bushed wristwise. But I won. *(They kiss carnivorously.)*

SONG   FELICITY: Conqueror.

                CASSIO: Faithful helpmeet.

                FELICITY: How's your wife?

                CASSIO: Fading fast.

                FELICITY: What's she on now?

                CASSIO: Poison capsules.

                FELICITY: These ought to be the last.

                CASSIO: Did you shine my wall of diplomas?

                FELICITY: Yes.

                CASSIO: And book some new carcinomas?

                FELICITY: No.

                CASSIO: Don't say it's the same old bland . . .

                FELICITY: Troubles? Yes, a tight wedding band,
Backaches, depressions, scratches, stings:
All the usual corny things.

                TOGETHER: The medical day is rarely picturesque
When you're stationed on this side of the desk.

FELICITY: We did get one typhoid.

CASSIO: Sounds good. Any chance of an outbreak?

CHORUS: *(Offstage)* Doctor, doctor, doctor, doctor: a pick me up, a lay me down, a relaxer, a laxative, a tonic, an emulsion, an astringent. Recharge me, sedate me, excite me. Anything to make life different.

CASSIO: They all paid up in advance?

FELICITY: Here. No checks, no records, no tax.

CASSIO: Any good will from the ethical drug corporations?

FELICITY: So so. Haven't counted it. I left it all in the envelopes. Two envelopes came empty.

CASSIO: I warned them about money through the mail. They want me to prescribe their lousy products, let em send the bribes by hand with the detail men.

FELICITY: The detail men keep stealing it and say they got mugged.

CHORUS: *(Offstage)* Doctor, doctor, doctor, doctor, feel me, heal me, seal me, deal me a new hand.

CASSIO: Fakes! I long for one sincere ailment. A patient is a distinctive face, a solo organism, a private world. We have to see you one at a time. What a curse, a bore. If it weren't for the money I'd go back to my first love, training bloodhounds.

CHORUS: Doctor, doctor, doctor, doctor, fix me good.

CASSIO: In the old days we gave you people the water cure, everybody at the same time, and let the weak ones drown. Okay, Felicity, sing em the overture.

FELICITY: The doctor is with you. He'll look at you, lay his hands on you, give you reassurance and a return appointment in three days. *(Cheers from offstage.)*

CASSIO: Felicity, suffer them to come unto me. *(FELICITY unlocks the waiting room door, keeping it chained, and opens it half an inch.)*

FELICITY: Easy, easy. You're squashing the old lady. The other old ladies are squashing her. Who's first? *(GARNISH crawls through. He has a shoe missing, tie in his mouth, pants up to his knees. FELICITY returns to her desk, organizes her lips.)* Name?

GARNISH: Soda T. Garnish.

FELICITY: What's the T for?

GARNISH: Temptation.

FELICITY: *(Writing on an idiot card)* New patient?

GARNISH: No.

FELICITY: Your three written referrals?

GARNISH: Some place here.

FELICITY: That'll be a supplemental fifty.

GARNISH: I said I have them.

FELICITY: That's why it's only fifty. You people, all you think of is saving nickels and dimes. You throw out money on food and clothes, then make a stink when it comes to important items like doctor payments.

GARNISH: I was about to recite a verse or two dedicated to your tempestuous forehead and wanton lips.

FELICITY: Don't suck up to me.

GARNISH: Lady, under this humble poet's custom-sewn alpinewear there lurks a bull elephant. If I loosened four leather buttons and lowered one zipper you'd be halfway to ecstasy.

FELICITY: Anyone can brag. *(He gives her money.)* See you after office hours.

GARNISH: I'll barely contain myself. *(Takes the idiot card in to* CASSIO.)

CASSIO: Garnish, eh? Newcomer, eh?

GARNISH: Haven't been in for six days, doctor. Forgive me, I was well.

CASSIO: As you know, then, I like to give patients what they ask for. Make it brief — people are dying out there.

GARNISH: I have this thing.

CASSIO: Speed up.

GARNISH: It's getting worse.

CASSIO: So?

CASSIO: Will I live?

CASSIO: Depends on how you survive the treatment.

GARNISH: What's the treatment?

CASSIO: What can you afford?

GARNISH: I don't want to stint when my health's at stake. A liquid?

CASSIO: *(Prescription pad ready)* Which one?

GARNISH: The red stuff?

CASSIO: Is that what you like?

GARNISH: I'll be candid. I prefer the orange.

CASSIO: *(Writing)* Orange stuff.

GARNISH: It tastes better. Maybe it's not so good?

CASSIO: We'll see. Come back in three days.

GARNISH: Will exercise hurt me?

CASSIO: Only in moderation.

GARNISH: Should I keep warm?

CASSIO: Why, do you feel cold?

GARNISH: Both.

CASSIO: Garnish, you better level with me.·

GARNISH: *(Cunningly)* In what way?

CASSIO: You're an investigator.

GARNISH: Try again.

CASSIO: Spying for my rivals in the medical arts building.

GARNISH: Two to me.

CASSIO: You're studying my style.

73

GARNISH: Three to me.

CASSIO: You're taking mental notes like crazy. *(He snatches off GARNISH's hair. Beneath it is a bald head.)*

GARNISH: I'll come clean with a grin that means: Forgive me for doing a Judas on you. Soda T. Garnish is an advertising poet. *(Snatches off the bald head. Beneath it is a crop of red hair.)* I devise copy that moves drugs off counters. I've cased your place. I like it. I'll dwell under your desk.

CASSIO: Not in a million years.

GARNISH: *(Offering a roll of bills)* From my employer.

CASSIO: Felicity, Mr. Garnish is staying. Put a cushion under my desk.

GARNISH: I am spinning with unusual rhymes like bug and drug. *(Sinks under desk with a cushion from FELICITY.)*

CASSIO: Next one in. *(FELICITY admits HARLOTTA, who stomps somebody behind her, stabs somebody else with her parasol.)*

FELICITY: *(To CASSIO)* It's your odalisque. Don't let her give you the business.

CASSIO: About her frigid husband?

FELICITY: I'll be at the keyhole.

CASSIO: I'll move her on.

HARLOTTA: *(Bursting into his sanctum)* Now, doctor, I feel curiously energetic. *(Exit FELICITY. HARLOTTA closes the door, pokes her parasol through the keyhole. FELICITY ducks.)*

CASSIO: Harlotta!

HARLOTTA: Cassio! *(They kiss brutally.)* Don't we have a historic doctor-patient relationship?

CASSIO: About your energy.

HARLOTTA: I'm an emotional landslide. I have the burning shivers.

CASSIO: So it's heat, not energy.

HARLOTTA: Cash, give me a merciless going-over. Omit nothing.

CASSIO: Yesterday you had an omit-nothing at home.

HARLOTTA: Yesterday — a lifetime away. You don't know how the pressure's been mounting.

CASSIO: So it's pressure, not heat.

HARLOTTA: It flies up and down my system. Cash, smother me with an old-fashioned examination. Quench my energy.

CASSIO: So it's energy, not pressure.

HARLOTTA: I hear scuffles.

CASSIO: In your head?

HARLOTTA: *(Coyly)* Lower down. Twitches, scampering.

CASSIO: You've swallowed a small animal. A stoat or a groundhog. This week the groundhogs are burying their nuts.

HARLOTTA: In me!

CASSIO: They find an old trunk and start to burrow.

HARLOTTA: For pity's sake, no more. Cash, hunt me up and down. Exterminate my wild game, the gnawing little animals. They won't let me rest. They're getting bigger. That's why I have this uncontrollable appetite.

SONG   HARLOTTA: Evenings I can put away a mile of tutti-fruitti,
Banana whips and chocolate thicks
And malted drecks and salted nuts.
Midnight comes,
The icebox is a dead hole in the wall,
I crawl around the floor and in the garbage bag
To snag potato peels or curling stinking melon rind
I find a lump of yellow fat
The cat forgot to finish
O I'll never again be thinnish,
I'll only bloat
Unless I learn to tame my inner stoat.

CASSIO: Have you stopped seeing your father?

HARLOTTA: Poppa was the greatest-looking hero I ever flashed a message at. But now he's moved out of my room.

CASSIO: He's back with your mother?

HARLOTTA: Don't talk to me about her. Cash, Cash, slim me down. Look into my wedgwood-blue eyes. In, in. Let your vision go wild.

CASSIO: *(Peering)* I've got it: a specialist!

HARLOTTA: Not a surgeon? *(He nods)* A surgeon! Am I worthy?

CASSIO: I don't know what he'll charge. I don't know how soon we can get him. Felicity, try to contact Dr. Knacker. *(FELICITY punches a button. ARTHUR comes in through the side door. He wears an eye-patch, chokes occasionally, and has a leg missing.)*

ARTHUR: *(Throwing his arms open)* Cash!

CASSIO: *(Joining the embrace)* Art!

ARTHUR: What's with the new yacht?

CASSIO: How was the world trip?

ARTHUR: Did you talk to my tailor?

CASSIO: You developing that property?

ARTHUR: Still accumulating antique cars?

CASSIO: What clubs you joining this year?

ARTHUR: How are your deductions?

CASSIO: You like the portfolio my broker recommended?

ARTHUR: Cash, you have a swell noise in that waiting room. How'd you do it?

CASSIO: Give em what they ask for.

ARTHUR: Me, I depend on my small, select clientele. I never give em what they ask for. I give em what they don't expect. They go for ritual. I burn a candle, a joss stick. Put on a tape, slice em about while they're listening. Brutality: it can't lose.

HARLOTTA: My, I like the sound of that.

CASSIO: Art, you've never met Harlotta.

ARTHUR: How the hell do I know who I've met? They come to me for communion, for punishment. It's dark, I can't see a fuckin' thing. The candle stinks, so does the joss stick. They want pain. I sock em with a jab and a yank. They're serious people.

CASSIO: Harlotta, Art Knacker is the fastest blade in the northeast.

ARTHUR: You name it, I'll remove it. Before you know it's gone.

CASSIO: A truly dedicated guy. Rehearses on himself.

ARTHUR: Any referral from Cash, it's gilt-edged. Do anything for him. He saved my life: cut me in on a fantastic stock option. Oil wells in the Bronx.

CASSIO: He saved my life too, more than once. Steered me away from a nineteen-oh-four Studebaker.

ARTHUR: You didn't notice it had worn tires.

CASSIO: Now, Art, Harlotta would like —

ARTHUR: Don't tell me what she'd like. I'll tell you what she's got to have.

HARLOTTA: That's what I like: what I've got to have. Shall I tell you what's wrong?

ARTHUR: I could diagnose it, but why waste time? Better: let me guess. Gnawing little animals.

HARLOTTA: Fantastic.

CASSIO: The only way to keep down their hunger is to feed em.

ARTHUR: Or starve em.

76

CASSIO: Or take em out.

ARTHUR: Naw, that's old hat. Today we figure out a total philosophy of clearance. I'm pondering. I'm going through a fierce internal debate.

CASSIO: Look at that. Any second now he'll strike oil.

HARLOTTA: Just so he doesn't send me away to a weight camp where they serve you food you have to throw up.

ARTHUR: How far are you over the line?

HARLOTTA: More than two and a half pounds.

ARTHUR: Two and a half whole pounds! Now I'm really pondering. Let's look at her from another angle. *(Harlotta starts to disrobe.)* Skip that. *(Stands on his head.)* I'd say the left shank is pretty flimsy.

HARLOTTA: Nobody ever criticized it before. Poppa used to go berserk over my left shank.

ARTHUR: Yes, the leg would take us most of the way. Five or six ounces to go. Fingers? Toes? Ears? Might not be enough. At this point most physicians would reduce intake.

CASSIO: Plenty of cabbage soup, Swedish crackers, and —

ARTHUR: Me, I'm not most physicians. I don't reduce intake, I reduce yearning. We yearn through our eyes, right? With one eye, her field of vision is restricted to one side of her nose. The optic nerve is exposed to fifty per cent less food. Not only do we halve the yearning: the food looks one-dimensional; it has less of a come-on.

HARLOTTA: I don't get it.

ARTHUR: Okay, one leg, one eye. We have our yearning beautifully diminished.

HARLOTTA: Maybe I do get it.

ARTHUR: Next step: we pop a virus into the lung. People with less lung tissue eat thriftily.

HARLOTTA: O God, do I get it!

CASSIO: A virus? I have three dozen grade one in this drawer. How do you introduce it into the lung?

ARTHUR: By hand, how else? You shove the goddam thing down her throat.

CASSIO: A virus is slippery to hold.

ARTHUR: I do it all the time. Did it to myself. It's all in the grip.

HARLOTTA: Keep arguing, the two of you. I'm listening and losing pounds.

ARTHUR: Cash, don't open a fresh package. I have a virus with me.

77

(Takes it from his pocket; holds it to the light.) Hi, feller. He's fine, healthy, plenty active. *(GARNISH comes out from under the desk.)*

GARNISH: How about this for a stopper? Everybody, listen.

CASSIO: Garnish, we have to get this surgery thing on the road. I have a roomful of dying patients out there.

GARNISH: I just completed a new head-cold poem. I'm about to recite it in my monotonous but sincere poet's delivery.

CASSIO: Not now, Garnish. We're operating.

GARNISH: I'm in my bathroom. I address my bloodshot image in the three-way mirror.

SONG   GARNISH: Your head starts to ring
It's trying to warn
Mornings at seven
Before you unfold
You swallow this thing
The day is reborn
God's in His heaven
All's right with your cold.

Is it a masterpiece? Will the Pulitzer crowd go gaga? *(Silence.)*

ARTHUR: Did I drop that goddam virus?

GARNISH: How could I expect appreciation from you scientific types? Browning, thou shouldst be living at this hour. Don't you follow? God's in His heaven. He's delighted. He belted down two ridiculously overpriced aspirins masquerading as time-released total coverage of the cold syndrome — and His day was reborn.

ARTHUR: False, false. He needed a leg ligature.

GARNISH: Between head-cold poems I'm doing a version of the Oedipus Tyrannus in Greek.

CASSIO: Isn't there already a version in Greek?

GARNISH: By Sophocles? I've seen it. It doesn't stand up.

RECITATIVE   Gentle ladies and gentlemen, for years
        I endured
Bleeding hemorrhoids of the conscience which
        they said could not be cured
How I squandered my lucky licence! — until
        the muse of tragedy
Crept into my bed one night and outlined
        a new strategy.
She gave me so much joy I recklessly made a

solemn promise
To keep my ad copy clean and classical, free
from misleading commas
And unsubstantiated claims, as well as
turgidity and triteness:
"Melpomene," I swore, "from now on I'm the
Homer of copywriteness,
"No longer will I produce those reams of
high-pressure, boastful, silly ads
"My reputation will stand or fall on
nothing less than iliads."

And now you understand, my friends, that in order to compose a believable head-cold poem I have to wallow in believable quantities of free-association phlegm. I can't write unless I sneeze what the customer sneezes. You saw through my earlier poem. It's dishonest, it's nonclassical, bordering on the neo-romantic, because I cannot seem to catch a cold. Help me . . .

CASSIO: Phlegm, he needs phlegm.

ARTHUR: Phlegm is unsurgical.

CASSIO: He's willing to pay for it.

ARTHUR: Well, a snoutful of phlegm, hey? We're talking about a slap-up operation with all the trimmings.

HARLOTTA: How do you operate for phlegm?

ARTHUR: Enthusiasm will find a way. The legs are a constant barrier against infection. I'm pondering again. Yes! This must be my day: a graceful delegging, genuine artistry, the Venus do Milo in reverse, with plenty of stump left in case he needs a repeat job.

CASSIO: Art, you're inspired.

ARTHUR: We mustn't forget the eyes. To a poet with a believable head cold, one watering eye has to be less of a handicap than two.

CASSIO: But you haven't given him a head cold.

ARTHUR: That's our final ploy: we tuck a hard-working virus into his lungs, and it drives all the phlegm into his head.

CASSIO: His head, that's something to think about. The head would take care of his eyes **plus** several adjacent organs. I say, compromise on the head.

ARTHUR: *(Feels GARNISH's head bumps.)* That's a new wrinkle. But fair enough. I'll settle for his head.

CASSIO: Felicity, the needle. A local anaesthesia.

FELICITY: We're out of needles. Will a funnel do?

79

ARTHUR: A funnel! Boy, I love funnels.

CASSIO: Where do we administer?

ARTHUR: In the adam's apple, where else? *(They arrange GAR-NISH neatly on the desk.)*

CASSIO: Funnel loaded?

FELICITY: To the gills.

CASSIO: I'll put it in quickly. I'm clever with funnels.

ARTHUR: Let me. I like the way they break the skin.

GARNISH: Procrastinators! *(Snatches the funnel and plunges it in his arm.)* Ooo . . .

ARTHUR: Look at him squirm. What did you put in the funnel?

FELICITY: A sixty-nine burgundy, modest but not unduly sweet.

ARTHUR: Montrachet?

FELICITY: Santenay.

CASSIO: Sixty-nine was an off-vintage year.

ARTHUR: I prefer Portuguese rosé for head operations.

CASSIO: Hit him with another jigger.

FELICITY: The whole bottle went through the funnel first time.

ARTHUR: He's bumpsy, barrelhouse. I'll decapitate him when he calms down, or he might grab one of my instruments. What do we have for a second shot?

FELICITY: Here's something. Mustard.

ARTHUR: Load it in and pile it high. We'll give him an oldtime mustard dressing.

GARNISH: Mustard hates me. I break out in yellow stripes. I get a split personality.

ARTHUR: My turn with the funnel. Aha!

GARNISH: Aaaa!

CASSIO: That mustard must have quite a tang.

FELICITY: It's the hot English kind.

ARTHUR: He crossed me up. He rolled aside. I inoculated the desk.

HARLOTTA: Poor thing. It looks groggy.

FELICITY: So would you if you had mustard trickling through your grain. *(GARNISH sits up and sneezes. He sneezes again. Again. He puts his finger horizontally under his nose; it doesn't help.)*

CASSIO: A sneezing jag — you didn't miss him.

ARTHUR: You know what this means? *(They embrace.)*

CASSIO: If we induced a head cold, we can induce anything: paralysis, alopecia, gangrene, warts . . .

ARTHUR: It's a new era in medicine.

CASSIO: No more futzing around with pimples and allergies and B-12 shots. We're in the bigtime.

HARLOTTA: Don't forget about me.

CASSIO: Some experiment: he came up with all the phlegm he can handle. Felicity, give him a tissue; he's messing up the floor.

FELICITY: It's the last one. Wipe, don't blow. *(GARNISH blows into it.)* I warned him. A good tissue and he had to ruin it.

GARNISH: Somebody want sumpn? Hey there, folks, any kinda thing you fancy.

FELICITY: He's still cooked.

CASSIO: Unless he's changed his personality.

ARTHUR: A temporary side effect.

HARLOTTA: You've killed the old him with mustard.

GARNISH: Anything you want: if it's a can-do I can do it.

CASSIO: Garnish, do you hear me?

GARNISH: Who's Garnish?

CASSIO: You're not?

GARNISH: Call me Ishmael.

CASSIO: He turned into fiction.

FELICITY: It's an act.

ISHMAEL: An act? What kind? You want some hot times, I'll heat. Sing, tap, soft shoe, ukulele, somersaults, ballads, billiards, trapeze, tightrope, the disappearing bedsheet, the galloping one-two, sawing a woman in half with a axe.

HARLOTTA: He's a wandering bloody minstrel.

ISHMAEL: You want minstrelsy, I'll minst. Epic, lyric, nostalgic. Mime, monologues, duologues . . . *(Puts on a doll glove.)*

GLOVE: Mr. Ish?

ISHMAEL: Yes, Mr. Bosh?

GLOVE: Let me in on the program for today.

ISHMAEL: The old game.

GLOVE: The imp cure, Mr. Ish?

ISHMAEL: The same, Mr. Bosh.

GLOVE: Not the little snatch?

81

ISHMAEL: The big snatch, if necessary.

GLOVE: Between these walls soothed down in green?

ISHMAEL: Lubricated by green.

GLOVE: This minute, Mr. Ish?

ISHMAEL: Whenever you're ready, Mr. Bosh.

SONG   GLOVE: Now take this one-eyed surgeon with the rolling
gimp
Or this general killer practitioner who's a
high-priced pimp
If he wants salvation
Why you snatch his imp
And set the little bastard free . . .
Now take this secretary who's a dried-out simp
Or this sleazy, greedy matron with the body
of a blimp
If she wants emaciation
Why you snatch her imp
And let the medication be . . .

ISHMAEL: A imp?

GLOVE: You bet.

ISHMAEL: Two imps?

GLOVE: Better yet.

ISHMAEL: All the imps that you can get?

GLOVE: We'll see.

(The GLOVE bows. ISHMAEL puts it away.)

HARLOTTA: Did you mean that? What you said about my weight?

ISHMAEL: Who, me?

HARLOTTA: You and your glove.

ISHMAEL: Mr. Bosh? He said a imp.

HARLOTTA: A imp? Is that what's gnawing at me?

ISHMAEL: He said so. A imp.

CASSIO: One moment.

HARLOTTA: No moments. Why shouldn't I have a imp? With that
iceberg lettuce for a husband. And I was ready to believe it was a
stoat.

ISHMAEL: A imp.

CASSIO: This discussion is repugnant and medieval.

ISHMAEL: You want to see it, lady?

HARLOTTA: Do I! My very own imp.

CASSIO: Art, are we going to allow this jester to fly in the face of medical science? In my office! *(ISHMAEL sweeps his hand across HARLOTTA's face.)*

ISHMAEL: There she is. A red and black beauty. She has a sharp tail and a fancy wiggle.

HARLOTTA: A she-imp. Wouldn't you know it? *(The others crowd around to look.)*

ARTHUR: A bona fide imp?

ISHMAEL: You want to hold her?

ARTHUR: Not me.

CASSIO: No, no! *(ISHMAEL opens the window, lets the imp go.)*

ISHMAEL: Look at her scuttle. Hustlin' off to find another home and lotsa T.L.C.

HARLOTTA: Stand back, I'm losing ballast. *(She rises into the air.)* I am the light of the world. I lost a imp.

CASSIO: It's a delusion. She only thinks she's up there.

ARTHUR: But you saw the imp. Didn't you?

CASSIO: Did you?

HARLOTTA: I love to be high where everybody can worship my ravishing new slimness.

ISHMAEL: How's about you, lady?

FELICITY: I'm underweight, not over. I **need** an imp. *(He passes his hand across her face.)*

ISHMAEL: Different color, this one. Yaller and green, sour as acid. Out the winder. Good huntin', honey. Funny durn thing. Cute's a kitten.

FELICITY: I feel strange. I must dance and spread love and go into social work. My bosom overflows with the milk of human kindness. Did I say milk? Make that half-and-half, even cottage cheese. *(She trips about throwing money, blowing kisses.)*

CASSIO: Art, if we don't run him out, he'll un-imp us all.

ARTHUR: Blood and feces, I'd be bolloxed. I don't have any imp, but if I did it would be my stock in trade.

HARLOTTA: *(Aloft)* I'm Harlotta. Come on and fly me.

FELICITY: *(Still distributing money)* There's fennel for you, and columbines. There's rue for you, and here's some for me. I'm not keeping a penny. It all goes to the United Fund. Anybody here like me to take over their illness? their surgery? Suffering for others is so beautiful.

ARTHUR: Cash, you've lost her. She turned into a saint.

CASSIO: This is as phony as the old water cure. Or leeches.

ARTHUR: Some of my clients enjoy a leech better than anything. Adds that finishing suck.

ISHMAEL: I hear you say sumpn about a water cure? Now?

CASSIO: He would, too. Quick, give him the bum's rush.

ARTHUR: Where to?

CASSIO: Anywhere. Before he does more damage here. *(They take ISHMAEL under each arm and facing backward; they propel him toward the waiting room.)*

ISHMAEL: Anybody wants me to wash away their imp, I'll wash.

CHORUS: A water cure, the water cure . . .

HARLOTTA: I want that too. Let me down. I want every cure going.

CHORUS: Water, water, water, the life of life, the miracle. Wash away our naiads and dryads and all the sprites that spite us. The water cure, the water cure.

CASSIO: He'll empty my waiting room. It's taken me twenty years to fill it. Patients don't trust a waiting room unless it's packed. *(ISHMAEL frees himself, takes out a divining rod and displays it in front of him. CASSIO and ARTHUR shrink from it.)*

ARTHUR: Cash, is something holding your arms?

CASSIO: Feels like an imp, if not a full-scale demon.

ISHMAEL: *(To the CHORUS)* Folks, I want you to see a picture of the water. A sunset on all the rivers of America when they slide along like pink glass.

ARTHUR: Fech, full of sewage.

CHORUS: The water cure, the water cure. We see the rivers inching into the ocean.

ONE VOICE: I can't see. Somebody's standing in my eyes. Ah, that's better: I blinked.

CHORUS: Deliver us from all imps. We see the water, we're in the water, we are the water.

ISHMAEL: Everybody say Ah.

CHORUS: Ahhh!

CASSIO: He stole that **ah** from orthodox medicine. Don't let him in-to my waiting room!

ISHMAEL: Come on out, you collective imp. *(Enters the waiting room.)* He's a biggie. Gotta use leverage. One, two, whip! That takes care a him. *(He reappears struggling with the collective imp. The CHORUS is singing, "We see the water, we're in the water, we are the water," as if marching. Their voices fade under the following lines.)*

ISHMAEL: Any a you folks like this collective imp to play with? No offers? *(Throws off the imp.)*

CASSIO: *(Struggling)* It jumped into my arms.

ARTHUR: Hold it fast.

CASSIO: I can't.

ARTHUR: *(Retreating)* Let it go.

CASSIO: I can't.

ISHMAEL: Treat it gentle. It's on'y a lost imp.

CASSIO: Get the thing off me.

ISHMAEL: It ain't holdin' you. Yer holdin' it.

HARLOTTA: Please, I want to come down now. For my water cure.

FELICITY: I'll cure you, dear lady. I'll lend you some of my good intentions.

ARTHUR: *(Struggling)* Goddammit, the thing's on me now. I — oof. It keeps striking below the belt with its spiky tail.

CASSIO: *(Struggling)* How can you have it? It's still on me.

ARTHUR: *(Struggling)* Ishmael, take it off.

CASSIO: *(Struggling)* Ishmael, please.

ISHMAEL: Yer frightening it. We'll let the poor displaced little crittur out the winder.

ARTHUR: *(Struggling)* Hurry, it's killing me. *(ISHMAEL goes toward him. He stops, sneezes, sneezes again.)*

CASSIO: *(Struggling)* Come on, come on, sneeze later.

ISHMAEL: Where's my pencil? Your prescription was brilliant. My head's as thick as a preposterously colorful figure of speech. I'm inspired.

CASSIO: *(Struggling)* It's Garnish. What happened to Ishmael?

GARNISH: Ishmael? He's in Moby Dick.

ARTHUR: *(Struggling)* In what?

GARNISH: My new novel. He's the narrator. It's the story of an overgrown imp of the sea. Science fiction with a vengeance. Well, back to my muse. *(Exit.)*

HARLOTTA: I want to come down, but I don't want to catch another dose of imps.

85

ARTHUR: *(Struggling)* I can't move toward the window.

CASSIO: *(Struggling)* It was a collective imp. Must have split up again. Where's Garnish? Where's Ishmael? Stop them. What happened to all those patients?

FELICITY: *(Still distributing cash like flowers)* All gone, all cured. Happy, happy day.

CASSIO: (Struggling) This is ridiculous. Imps are a pre-medical superstition.

(ARTHUR and CASSIO continue to struggle. FELICITY skips around. HARLOTTA looks down longingly.)

THE END

The Seizure

YOSEF, youngish
HERMAN, middle-aged
EMIL, oldish
SIGRID, very young
WILLI, young and small
MOTHER, the oldest, out of it

YOSEF: *(Offstage)* Sigrid! Seeegrid! *(Enters.)* Beloved, angel. To me, Sigrid, itch of my life, my Venus, my sunburst, my heart's target. My friend. *(WILLI crosses, walking backward and dragging his jacket by the collar. YOSEF watches him. WILLI goes off.)* Sigrid, before it gets dark. Hurry to me, gallop, fly, crawl, you serpent. O my Sigrid. *(He hugs an imaginary body, kisses an imaginary face.)* Before it's too late, Sigrid. I warn you: I'll take any rock in this desert, any cactus, and give it everything I've got. Circle your Yosef, muffle me, plough me under. Sigrid, I can't wait, it's dinner time. I'll write you a nourishing love letter. *(HERMAN enters down the middle, counting his paces. He marks the ground.)* Herman, what rhymes with Sigrid?

HERMAN: I'm counting. *(Exit right.)*

YOSEF: Fleagrid? Eegrid? *(HERMAN returns from the right.)* What's an eegrid? Help me out.

HERMAN: Eleven, twelve, thirteen. *(He makes a mark that intersects the first.)*

YOSEF: I'm in this fix. It's now or never. Any second.

HERMAN: There she is.

YOSEF: She is?

HERMAN: Our hot center. Our dead center. *(Bends his knees, puts an index finger on the center and goes around it drawing a circle with his other index finger.)*

YOSEF: Not bad for a center. Interesting, mysterious, colorful. Except I have my own center to worry about. *(Howls.)* Sigrid, dear vessel, into you I will spill my longing. *(Wanders.)*

HERMAN: Don't go, Yosef, now we have a circle.

YOSEF: Circles remind me of my solitude. I'll go out of my skin if I don't find her.

HERMAN: Everything fair, orderly, organized. Each of us will have his own place on the circumference with a share of the fire at our center.

YOSEF: Piss on it. I don't mean that. It's my anguish talking.

HERMAN: Everyone will sit a fair and equal radius from the heat. *(WILLI re-enters, right, dragging his jacket. They watch. He goes off left.)*

HERMAN: Everybody must respect the radius. Sit, kneel, stoop, you have your choice. Some people like their ass smack up against a fire. Not here. No favoritism.

YOSEF: Can I have the next radius to Sigrid?

HERMAN: We'll play chess for it.

YOSEF: Better — Sigrid and I can share a single radius. That'll leave more radii for the others.

HERMAN: Nothing doing. One radius each. In this community we go for equality, the more the better, an overpowering amount. You'll have your portion of the heat, Sigrid hers.

YOSEF: I want her to have mine.

HERMAN: Here, Yosef, I need you.

YOSEF: I'm busy.

HERMAN: I want you.

YOSEF: *(Approaching)* That's more like it.

HERMAN: Take over the center for me. Guard it.

YOSEF: Couldn't you place that center somewhere less exposed? In a sheltered spot, a nooky shelter?

HERMAN: Stand right on it: great. Now nobody can trespass.

88

YOSEF: Herman, I don't like centers. They make me dizzy.

HERMAN: I'll be back.

YOSEF: From where?

HERMAN: Don't budge. Keep your eyes on the circle. *(YOSEF takes a step to one side and two back.)*

YOSEF: I'm a knight. Help, I'm lost, I'm eccentric.

HERMAN: *(Restoring him to the center)* You're the sentry. *(With a fist under his nose.)* I nominate you.

YOSEF: Where am I? Where are the others?

HERMAN: Looking for a shipwreck. *(Exit.)*

YOSEF: If I found a shipwreck I'd hide it. *(Calling)* Herman, I don't like the climate here. Or the ambiance. I feel attackable. Reinforce me with a Sigrid or two. *(Steps off the center and warms his hands at it.)* Fire? O mother, the wind will brush it all out to sea. I know this wind. Wicked. It's fanning my lust. Squeezing me into a horn-backed toad. My soul is hanging out. Mother, mother, look down from your heavenly campfire. Have pity on your boy, rotted by lust and hounded by winds.

MOTHER: *(12 feet above ground, sticking through a curtain)* Give thanks for the wind and all other things that blow.

YOSEF: Mother, look how I'm situated. Between water and water. An island, of all settings. A tempest could blow it away. One suit of emotions I have and not a thing to put into it. If we'd thought of bringing more Sigrids. Twice as many Sigrids as men. Six, a thousand times as many. With vast numbers of Sigrids we could have made something of this landscape. I could roam these parts cushioned by a thousand Sigrids. Mother, I don't trust these parts. There are not enough of them. *(WILLI drags his jacket by. He rests, wipes his face.)*

WILLI: Quiet today.

YOSEF: Willi, what are you hauling there?

WILLI: Rocks.

YOSEF: From the beach?

WILLI: From all over.

YOSEF: Impressive rocks?

WILLI: Rocks.

YOSEF: With different surfaces and shapes and sizes?

WILLI: Plain rocks.

YOSEF: It's a terrific idea.

WILLI: You think so?

YOSEF: Collecting something as serious as rocks. Handling them with love. Which do you pick? The ones with veins, hearts, big passions?

WILLI: All of em.

YOSEF: Are they pairs? Male and female?

WILLI: Some are.

YOSEF: Having a great time mating them up?

WILLI: Back to work.

YOSEF: Wish I could give you a hand and really step up the enjoyment.

WILLI: I'll manage.

YOSEF: Too bad I'm pinned down here at the center.

WILLI: So long.

YOSEF: If somebody spelled me . . . for a few seconds . . .

WILLI: *(Leaving)* Yeah.

YOSEF: Willi, what the hell are you up to with those rocks?

WILLI: The usual, you know. Building a line.

YOSEF: A line of pavement? A line of progress?

WILLI: That sort of thing. *(Exit.)*

YOSEF: What if she doesn't come? How will I deal with this hunger? I'll fight it. I'll dream about an egg. Did you hear that, Willi?

WILLI: *(Offstage)* What?

YOSEF: A fat, luscious, uncooked egg, all wet and snotty, heavy with cholesterol. Because eggs are basic. I'm dreaming. I'm letting my mouth fill with saliva. Salivary glands going like suction pumps. Mouth dripping. Hardly talk. *(Swallows.)* I'm spooning egg past my anxious teeth. Mouth is awash again. Gulp. Into the esophagus. Gathering speed. Plop. Landed four-square in the stomach. Piling up against the pyloric sphincter. More, where? I didn't taste the yolk. What happened? Don't say I came up with a yolkless egg? *(Running his tongue around his cheeks.)* There you are, you little yellow creep . . Hiding, wearing a mask. Willi, I found it: the yolk of yolks. I hope you live to bury a sunny yolk of that caliber in your innards. The experience! It's pouring through my body. I'm all yolk. O Sigrid! *(EMIL enters.)* Emil, rescue me.

EMIL: Yosef, you know where I went? Out of our boundaries.

YOSEF: Some boundaries. Sand, water.

90

EMIL: You want to see?

YOSEF: Sure, take my place. Center your life. Standing here is one of those all-time feelings.

EMIL: I'm no good at standing. Hey, I investigated the bird population. Piping plovers. Or rather, sanderlings. Unless they were puffins. Won't commit myself on that. Possibly seagulls, the herring kind. Or gannets. Definitely gannets now I think about it. Gannets or shearwaters. I found an egg, a giant seagull egg. Or gannet.

YOSEF: A real egg? I'm fainting for an egg. Emil, bless you.

EMIL: I ate it.

YOSEF: Uncooked? That's primitive.

EMIL: I'm supposed to eat eggs.

YOSEF: Me too.

EMIL: But they give me dreams.

YOSEF: Serves you right, you egg hog.

EMIL: Did I actually eat it? Took it in my hand . . . made a firm decision . . . brooded . . . rejected original plan . . . No.

YOSEF: You didn't? Good old Emil.

EMIL: It's still here in my pocket.

YOSEF: An authentic egg with a sensuous great yolk! What will you take for it? I'll give you my radius, my share of the boundaries. We'll fry it on a rock, the way eggs taste best.

EMIL: Look at that. It broke.

YOSEF: You muffed up my only egg?

EMIL: It's flowing over my lining. Hold out your hands, I'll trickle it to you. Or should I let it dry out and harden into a negotiable lump? Oops, it fell. *(Wipes fingers on YOSEF's shirt.)*

YOSEF: No egg. Where's Sigrid?

EMIL: You know what this island's made up of?

YOSEF: She's the eggiest thing that could happen to me.

EMIL: Rock.

YOSEF: Rocks?

EMIL: Plain rock.

YOSEF: What were we thinking of when we talked about a promised land? How do you found a community on rock?

EMIL: I did some quick figuring. The sea will take roughly a million and a half years to wash away rock this durable.

YOSEF: How do you raise children on bare rock? And where's

Sigrid?

EMIL: It's not bare. It has topsoil. Very thin and brittle, mostly sand. I'd say the original inhabitants must have enjoyed wonderful grazing on topsoil this thin and brittle.

YOSEF: Where are they now?

EMIL: What thrives on pastures?

YOSEF: Farmers.

EMIL: Little, hardy sheep. They graze, they digest, they crap it out. In no time flat you have a flourishing heap of humus. From there you can go anywhere. Now, the horses —

YOSEF: Sheep.

EMIL: Or goats, because shit is versatile. The goats yield goat-foot jelly, horns, glue from the hooves. Besides which, goats make friendly pets. Miniature goats, the size of chihuahuas. You don't tell em about the glue plan.

YOSEF: For pets I prefer canaries; you can't eat goats. Their flesh tastes like nylon.

EMIL: Forget your gut for a minute.

YOSEF: How? My gut is me.

EMIL: I'm trying to put us into a perspective and tie us up with history.

YOSEF: I'm all molten inside. What's with Sigrid?

EMIL: Who?

YOSEF: Your daughter.

EMIL: Oh, that Sigrid.

YOSEF: I'll give her everything I have, right here at our center.

EMIL: My Sigrid is destined for bigger things.

YOSEF: Bigger than me?

EMIL: I've mapped out her future. We'll do research together. That's how we've always been, Sigrid and I, a community of scholars.

YOSEF: I'm a driven man, compelled to lead her into forbidden joys.

EMIL: If you touch my Sigrid.

YOSEF: I'll touch her. I'll never stop touching her. We'll meet, stand paralyzed. It'll be love at first sight and madness unto death.

EMIL: I'll cut your tongue out.

YOSEF: That won't stop me.

EMIL: I have this spoon; I sharpened up the edge; I'm striking a dangerous pose.

WILLI: *(Offstage)* Stay off my line.

EMIL: What line's he talking about?

WILLI: *(Offstage)* You're on it. Get off. *(EMIL moves.)*

EMIL: I sharpened the edge. But not too sharp. A blunt edge is more painful.

YOSEF: O mother, he's after my tongue.

MOTHER: Listen, women are poison. I speak as your mother, a neutral party.

YOSEF: But I'm sold on Sigrid. I have this gigantic thing for her.

EMIL: When you saw her twenty minutes ago you didn't tell her about any gigantic thing.

YOSEF: I forgot.

MOTHER: Never explain, son, never apologize.

EMIL: I'll divide your gigantic thing into teaspoonfuls. *(HERMAN returns carrying driftwood.)*

HERMAN: Make way for the fire.

YOSEF: Can I still move? Do I function? Shall I dare to step out into the world? *(Springs away from the center.)* Liberty! I can go anywhere! *(Sits, falls asleep.)*

EMIL: What's that, Herman, flotsam and jetsam?

HERMAN: About forty-sixty. The jetsam is magnificent, like cabinetwood, hand-rubbed. It'll really burn.

EMIL: I forgot something. *(Exit.)*

HERMAN: *(Laying the driftwood)* Smack in the center. A perfect distribution of warmth. *(Twirls one stick in the knothole of another.)* Nothing. *(Feels the stick; burns himself.)* Where can I get an oil-soaked rag?

EMIL: Here. *(Drags a grandfather clock into sight.)* Know where this came from?

HERMAN: Do you have an oil-soaked rag?

EMIL: Out of the sea. Still ticking away. *(Pats the clock on the shoulder.)* An ancestral type. My type. My daughter would love it. *(YOSEF opens his eyes.)* I'll give it to her if she never marries. I think the sea rejuvenated it.

YOSEF: I've been dreaming. *(Gets up, embraces the clock, kisses its face, pumps his belly against it.)*

EMIL: You grandfather-fouler. I think of my daughter, and —

YOSEF: I think of nothing else. *(Kisses the clock again, steps back, studies it critically.)*

EMIL: Take your filthy eyes off my ancestor.

YOSEF: Old age is repulsive.

MOTHER: What?

YOSEF: Mothers excepted.

MOTHER: I should hope so.

EMIL: What's repulsive about that sturdy, upright posture? Characteristically quattrocento. He's smiling: it's ten minutes to two.

YOSEF: You call that posture? He has no arms.

EMIL: Would you want arms if you had a pair of hands like that on your face? And what a face: the expression. The numerals have a quaint twelfth-century charm. Look at that VIII.

YOSEF: I prefer the X. It's shorter.

EMIL: He's Italian or Persian. Visigothic, something in that style. Franco-Prussian sort of thing. Armenian . . . or Tasmanian. I'm really attached to him. He's me in wood. The natives couldn't find enough topsoil for crops so they grew clocks. This one was their god of gods.

YOSEF: The god of love.

EMIL: That's right, Apollo.

YOSEF: Mercury.

EMIL: Lead.

YOSEF: Magnesium.

EMIL: Hydrogen peroxide.

YOSEF: Let's drink to that.

EMIL: Let's kneel to it. *(They kneel.)*

HERMAN: A wooden idol! We'll smash him up. I'm short of kindling. He'll make us a bonfire. A pillar of flame. Not high enough for a signal: we don't want passing ships to leave the horizon and spirit us away. We'll create a tremendous little pillar of fire, shedding the same ration of heat on everybody.

EMIL: Burn the grandfather of us all? That would be collective suicide.

YOSEF: I'm famished. O mother.

MOTHER: Have a sandwich. *(Tosses one down.)*

HERMAN: *(Drawing back his fist)* One punch in the throat will do it. We'll have him in splinters.

YOSEF: *(Eating)* Mother, your sandwiches are terrible. They close up my throat.

EMIL: Don't strike him.

YOSEF: Burn him whole. It's less agony than splintering. Anyway, splinters don't give out much heat.

EMIL: I love this old man. Anybody tries to harm one splinter of his head . . .

YOSEF: Mother, this bread is off. It's dead bread. *(Throws away the sandwich.)*

WILLI: *(Offstage)* Keep your garbage off my line.

YOSEF: Not my fault; it bounced.

MOTHER: This one is more fresh. I had it in cellophane wrap. *(She tosses him a second sandwich.)*

YOSEF: *(Takes a bite.)* Fit to burn.

HERMAN: Everybody says burn. Who has matches?

YOSEF: Nobody has a thing. Was I ever so destitute?

MOTHER: Matches? Safety matches? *(Tosses a box of matches to YOSEF. HERMAN takes them. He strikes one after another against the clock, against the kindling. He strikes one against his shirt. It catches fire. He smothers it.)*

HERMAN: The wind will finish our flame unless we gather in a tight circle.

EMIL: I could call Sigrid and the others.

YOSEF: Did you have to mention her provocative name? I was just getting over my hunger. Those sandwiches . . .

EMIL: I'm going to see my Sigrid and the others again! *(Going to the wings)* Sigrid! Others! Sigrid!

WILLI: *(Offstage)* Don't lean over my line.

EMIL: An accident. Sigrid! *(SIGRID steps out of the clock.)*

HERMAN: What happened to the others?

SIGRID: Some of the others said they saw them.

HERMAN: Emil, check out the inside of the clock.

SIGRID: Who cares about them?

EMIL: Fewer mouths to eat.

HERMAN: To eat? To feed.

SIGRID: Not cannibalism? Don't say that. How exciting.

EMIL: Daughter, what did you discover?

SIGRID: I went over the island inch by inch. It appears to be a peninsula.

YOSEF: Sigrid, at last. Is this how dreams come true? In twenty minutes how did she change so drastically? She grew. She filled out every which way. I'm blind and drunk and the music of the spheres pounds in my chest. Dreams are nothing. *(The lights dim. YOSEF and SIGRID are spotlit; the others remain still and dark.)* Now for the moment. How can I face her without revealing what I feel? Reveal, then, reveal. To a girl like Sigrid? She'd be disgusted. Sigrid, Sigrid, shall I tell you the truth?

SIGRID: If you phrase it colorfully.

YOSEF: What happened to your hair?

SIGRID: I cut it.

YOSEF: Poor darling. Did it hurt?

SIGRID: A thin and trim and set. I improvised with a shell.

YOSEF: You shaved off your mustache.

SIGRID: I may let it grow again.

YOSEF: The sea air should help.

SIGRID: If we're on a peninsula that would make the sea more of a lagoon.

YOSEF: A lagoon! Blue heaven and you and I.

SIGRID: In which case we belong to a continental land mass.

YOSEF: Sigrid, will you run away with me across this continental land mass?

SIGRID: Not if it's an island.

YOSEF: If it's an island will you swim away with me?

SIGRID: I doubt it.

YOSEF: There must be a powerful reason.

SIGRID: Now my hair's new I'm a whole different person. I only hope I reach my sixteenth birthday unscarred by acne.

YOSEF: Your sarong, Sigrid, it overwhelms me. It suits your buttocks.

SIGRID: This is what everybody's doing with buttocks lately.

EMIL: Sigrid, pay me some attention.

(The lights snap on.)

YOSEF: Mother, mother, you see that tantalizing thing she did to her second-best feature?

MOTHER: It's a woman's way to fight nature.

EMIL: Daughter, did you bring me back any conclusive research?

SIGRID: I dug up this beer can.

EMIL: Never forgets her father. The training is everything. *(Takes can.)* You slut. The can is open. It's full of sea.

SIGRID: Lagoon.

EMIL: I hate the taste of lagoon. *(Drops can.)*

WILLI: *(Offstage)* Get that can of lagoon off my grid.

YOSEF: Now he's weaving his line into a grid.

HERMAN: We need a grid. One rectangle per person. With a fire in the circle to soften the geometry.

YOSEF: When are you going to light that fire, instead of forecasting it? We could bake a potato, roast a marshmallow, so we feel like Christmas.

HERMAN: Did I see an oil-soaked rag?

EMIL: That was Yosef.

WILLI: *(Offstage)* Clear my zone. There's a zone either side of my grid.

YOSEF: That Willi, he knows where he is. He gives me confidence. I'm packed with electricity. Every two of my bones touch and give off lightning. Sigrid, is any of my voltage reaching you?

SIGRID: What color is it? What flavor? I may re-do my ears.

YOSEF: Mother, come in fast. Fertilize my hopes. What's the word from on high?

MOTHER: Stay clear of that young bitch, you hear your mother talking? I'm not prejudiced.

HERMAN: Let's rally ourselves. We came here to escape fragmentation, to stop the drift into entropy. We handpicked ourselves. We must consolidate.

HERMAN, EMIL, YOSEF: This is to be my rectification. I go back, write footnotes into my past, correct the mistakes there.

HERMAN: Relive.

YOSEF: Revise.

EMIL: Revive.

HERMAN, EMIL, YOSEF: Refuse the bad dreams that dog me, wash out all that's over and defective.

EMIL: I want to focus now on then.

YOSEF: I want to now all my thens.

HERMAN: If we light a fire.

HERMAN, EMIL, YOSEF: A fire, a new beginning . . .

SIGRID: Golden eyelashes, that's the answer. From six feet they're invisible, from six inches, inescapable.

YOSEF: *(Reaching for her)* While there's time, Sigrid, you and I, right here. A bud, a branch, a family tree.

EMIL: *(Drawing her back)* While there's time, Sigrid, you and I. A notion, a sequence, a grand theory. Right here, imprinted on the rock of ages.

YOSEF: Go down, you sunset; make way for the coming day.

EMIL: Ripen up, cucumber; you're still green behind the pits.

YOSEF: Sigrid . . .

EMIL: Sigrid . . .

SIGRID: I've been wondering. How would a bang look? Kind of sacred, no? Running two-thirds of the width across my forehead and taking possession of one temple?

YOSEF: She's saying she loves me, talking in symbols.

EMIL: How's this for a symbol? *(He whips out his spoon.)*

YOSEF: Mother, he's caught me spoonless.

MOTHER: Foil him. Here. I didn't have time to fine-grind it, but it'll cut. *(She whips out a spoon, tosses it to YOSEF who catches it by the hilt, examines the blade, grunts his approval. With much flexing of knees and elbows the two men move into en garde positions. SIGRID strikes down the two spoons. The duelists circle, feint, close in, engage. [The contest opens behinds HERMAN's following speech.] They are both fluent, virtuoso spoonsmen. The duel demonstrates EMIL's superior cunning and practice with the weapons. He tricks YOSEF several times, and the fight seems to be going his way. He achieves several palpable hits. He laughs. But YOSEF, by virtue of his youth, agility, and lack of arthritis, as well as the nap he took earlier in the action, recovers. At one point he gets EMIL at his mercy by unspooning him. He seems reluctant to wound EMIL, and looks sheepishly at SIGRID. As he does, EMIL bounds forward, kicks YOSEF in the stomach, regains his spoon from the sandy topsoil, and takes refuge behind a flashing display of parries and evasions, which hold off YOSEF's angry, pressing fleche attack.)*

HERMAN: A fire? No. Fires eventually smolder. We need an act of overriding communication. A bridge! Not a lumpy girderish tunnel, a sewer on legs, but a cobweb, filigree, arching above us. A lift for the heart, an intermittence, a highway to take us out of ourselves. It will extend . . . in all directions. What is the definitive feature of a bridge?

Its middle, its crossing point. Most bridges take shape at the extremities. Not ours. Ours will grow outward from a trustworthy middle. And we'll found the middle directly over our center. Up there. A sturdy curve. Anchored, braced with T-frames. Offering capacity to unlimited lanes of traffic . . . in all directions. Trucks with trailers, bicycles, excursion busses with a washroom under every seat, footpaths, shopping malls, forests, mountains, airports, battleships. And us. A bridge with such a configuration isn't ashamed to say *(In a bridge voice)*, "I soar, yet I belong rooted in your lives. I am a bridge."

EMIL: A bridge! *(The word spurs him on. YOSEF trips, falls.)*

YOSEF: Mother, strengthen this hand!

MOTHER: It was always your nicer hand. The first look I got at you I pointed out to the head nurse, "That hand is handsome compared with the other one."

YOSEF: But mother!

EMIL: Screw your mother.

YOSEF: Say that again.

EMIL: Screw your mother twofold. *(YOSEF comes to his feet in a fury and reverses the odds.)*

HERMAN: It will be a product of the most advanced engineering principles. A bridge with no visible or invisible means of support. *(YOSEF drives his spoon into EMIL. EMIL drops. YOSEF and SIGRID stare at each other. Their faces express concurrent remorse, horror, love, fear, triumph, and seven or eight other feelings.)* Of course we have to get it up there in the first place. We'll need hundreds of thousands of rocks.

WILLI: *(Offstage)* No rocks left.

HERMAN: A couple of armfuls, eh, Willi? A loan. We'll hand them back as soon as the bridge is up.

WILLI: *(Offstage)* Not a chance.

HERMAN: One rock — to start us off?

WILLI: *(Offstage)* Not one.

HERMAN: One of your spares.

WILLI: The spares go into my pile.

HERMAN: Willi, you have lines, grids, piles. Couldn't we borrow one of your piles? *(No answer.)* Willi!

YOSEF: Sigrid, my attitude toward you hasn't changed. Your father is not dead, except in the technical sense. But what can I do to make up for the loss?

SIGRID: Give me a baby.

YOSEF: I don't have a baby to give.

MOTHER: If it was anybody but my boy asking. *(She throws down a baby.)*

YOSEF: *(Catching it)* I never saw one of these before. Sigrid, you sure this is what you want?

SIGRID: It's what every woman wants.

YOSEF: Here, then. *(Throws her the baby.)*

SIGRID: The little godsend. *(She drops it.)* I was never much as a catcher. My forte is batting. *(Picking it up)* Shall I bat it back?

YOSEF: Not to me. It's sticky.

SIGRID: Looks as if the fall dented it on top.

HERMAN: It resembles your late father.

SIGRID: Maybe. I don't recall his features as an infant. Ah, those teeny ears, those shells . . .

YOSEF: Real shells?

SIGRID: Would my baby have anything that was fake? And the eyes, the fingers. You know, the eyes are small even for a baby. Oops. *(She drops the baby again.)*

YOSEF: Did you crack it?

SIGRID: Who knows? I think a hairline crack or two. What can you do? Babies crack easier than eggs.

HERMAN: Pitch it to me. Babies like my calm manner.

SIGRID: I'll bat it. *(Picks it up.)* I don't feel confident about my pitching arm. *(She bats the baby. And misses it.)* My game is off today.

HERMAN: *(Gathering it up)* A newborn. Verging on mankind. Our greatest achievement, innocence, even if innocence is behind the times. By God, it **is** gummy. Anybody have a tissue with some alcohol on it? *(Flings the baby off his fingers. It lands near EMIL. He pushes it alongside with his foot.)* It's your descendant all right, old friend. Your physique, your disposition. If we had our bridge I could see the two of them striding it, arm in arm, captains of us all. They'd have smelled the sky, reported back on its perfume. Go ahead, tell me I'm a sentimental slob. What do you know about life if you don't give in to your weaknesses at least once every hour? *(Weeping)* Weeping testifies to our humanity. *(He breaks down. The clock chimes the hour. He perks up.)* Midday. Or midnight. Another beginning.

YOSEF: O mother, I'm sick of beginnings.

MOTHER: They're like winds. Part of the evolutionary cycle thing.

HERMAN: Emil, I can feel blood waves pulsing between you and your grandson. You would have wanted me to perform a ceremony. Approach me, you two . . . lovebirds!

SIGRID: A wedding. The baby will adore it.

YOSEF: Hold on! Who wants her now? A baby, it means one more mouth to eat.

SIGRID: To feed.

YOSEF: Besides, I've gone off her.

SIGRID: I don't believe it. He's dumping me and the baby on an endless peninsula?

YOSEF: Who's she to talk? A jar that's unstoppered, a bitten plum.

HERMAN: Yosef, she's yours. Step toward me, both of you.

SIGRID: Who takes the baby?

YOSEF: Not me. It's still sticky.

HERMAN: *(Giving it to him)* We'll wash it off with lagoon.

YOSEF: She asked for it, not me.

SIGRID: Its skin is all scabby . . . It'll ruin my white organdy.

HERMAN: Come, you nest of doves. Receive my blessing unless any man has objections . . . ?

YOSEF: I —

HERMAN: Other than the groom.

WILLI: *(Offstage)* You're on my zone.

HERMAN: Dearly beloveds, let us move off his zone. *(They shift.)*

WILLI: *(Offstage)* You're on my bullseye.

YOSEF: You said it was a grid, a pile.

WILLI: *(Offstage)* Off it. *(They shift.)*

HERMAN: In the name of the father, the son-in-law, and —

WILLI: *(Offstage)* You're edging into my other zone. *(They run to a far corner, YOSEF holding the baby.)* Grid! *(They run to the opposite corner.)* Pile! *(They run to a third corner.)* Bullseye! *(They stop, exhausted.)*

HERMAN: His bullseye — what is it? A slum.

YOSEF: O mother.

MOTHER: I'm here, my little one. But you're there.

YOSEF: Do me a favor: take this back. We're not ready for it. *(He throws her the baby.)*

MOTHER: *(Catching it)* You didn't even ask was it a boy or a girl. *(She vanishes behind the curtain.)*

YOSEF: Emil, Emil, I should have shown restraint. Now more than ever we could use your fatherly character.

EMIL: *(Raising his head briefly)* Return to this? Lines? Zones? Piles? Illegitimacy? Not on my life.

HERMAN: Willi, you can't skulk there out of sight forever. There's one of you to three of us, plus the stern corpse. Creep in here if you dare. Meet us nose to nose. *(They wait, grim. WILLI enters putting on his jacket.)*

HERMAN: And now —

WILLI: Silence! It's mine, every pile, every zone, the entire grid, every bullseye of it is mine. Mine by trigonometry, by conveyancing, effort and simple addition.

HERMAN: The insect. Tread on him.

YOSEF: He's fast on his feet.

HERMAN: Stone him.

YOSEF: He has the rocks, all of them.

HERMAN: Spring at him.

YOSEF: He's taken the ground, all of it. *(WILLI advances, takes SIGRID.)* He's got Sigrid, the whole of her.

HERMAN: Do something. *(WILLI stands between SIGRID and the clock. He inhales, then blows HERMAN and YOSEF offstage.)*

WILLI: Mine.

THE END

LEARNING RESOURCES

CENTER

ILLINOIS CENTRAL COLLEGE
MCMLXVI

East Peoria, Illinois

AVAILABLE POSTPAID FROM ORACLE PRESS

American Men's Wear, 1861-1982, by Wm. Harlan Shaw. What the American man has worn to work, to party, to play, from 1860 to the present. Specifically for the costumer, but with appeal to the general reader. Approximately 80 pages of text and 500 photos. 8½ × 11, typeset. $21.50. Publication date of 1 Oct. 1982.

Corrugated Scenery, by Briant Hamor Lee and Daryl Wedwick. A practical, how-to manual on inexpensive and workable scenery and props. Approximately 100 pages with nearly 90 black and white illustrations. 8½ × 11, spiral binding. Ideal for the workshop. $10.50. Publication date of 1 Oct. 1982.

Genealogy To Enrich the Curricula, by Frances Holloway Wynne and Cj Stevens. The uses of genealogy to bolster the teaching of English, history, art, and other disciplines at the junior high school level. For the teacher. 100 pages with charts and illustrations. 8½ × 11, spiral bound for easy desk use. $12.50. Publication date of 1 Oct. 1982.

Six One-Act Farces, by Albert Bermel. Six witty, modern one-acters from the pen of the distinguished New York City critic and playwright. The plays are attuned to today's audiences, players, and stage. Typeset, 6 × 9, perfect binding, 100 pp. $9.95. Publication date of 1 Oct. 1982.

Phaedra and *Iphigenia,* translations by Dr. William L. Crain of two of Racine's classic dramas, retaining the imagery and music of Racine's poetry. Eminently playable on the modern stage. Introduction by Dr. Patricia McIlrath. 6 × 9, typeset, approximately 150 pages. $16.00. Publication date of 1 Oct. 1982.

Three Plays by Louisiana Playwrights. Full evening-length plays: "Savonarola," a powerful historical drama by Perry Guedry; "The Isle of Barrataria," a verse adaptation of Royal Tyler's play, by Cj Stevens; "Callie's Boy," a musical comedy based on the life of young Huey Long, by George C. Brian. 6 × 9, offset, 228 pages. $15.00. Publication date of 1 Oct. 1982.

All' Italiana, by Rosaria di Lucente Bhacca. A gourmet Italian cookbook which takes into consideration American eating habits, tastes, and ingredients. Offset edition: $6.95. Typeset: $7.95.